MW01598924

CONNECTED GROUNDED AND *Guided*

Parenting Spiritually in the Digital World

JEB J. BERSABAL

Printed in U.S.A.

Published by
Jabez Ministry and Mentors International

Unless otherwise indicated, all scripture quotations are taken
from various versions available for public use on biblegateway.com.

ISBN: 978-1-966929-17-8

Editor : Sarah Green
Cover Photo : Ramsey Dawson
Cover Design & Layout : Haley Trimmer

DEDICATION

Dear God,

With heartfelt gratitude, I dedicate my book, "Connected, Grounded, and Guided - Parenting Spiritually in the Digital World," to You. You are the ultimate source of wisdom, guidance, and grace, and it is through Your strength that this book has come to fruition. May it serve as a beacon of light and inspiration to families seeking to navigate the challenges of the digital age with faith and resilience.

To my beloved family,

You are my rock, my support, and my inspiration. This book is a testament to the love and devotion we share, and it is dedicated to each of you. May its message of connection, grounding in faith, and guidance through God's Word strengthen our bond and inspire us to grow together in love and spiritual growth.

To my dear friends,

Your encouragement, prayers, and unwavering support have been a constant source of strength throughout this journey. I am grateful for your friendship and companionship. This book is dedicated to you, with the hope that its message will resonate with your hearts and enrich your lives as it has mine.

ACKNOWLEDGMENT

I would like to express my heartfelt gratitude to the following individuals whose invaluable contributions made the creation of this book possible:

Dr. Armand T. Fabella

As one of the editors and the author of the foreword, your expertise and insights into family dynamics—particularly parent-child relationships—greatly enriched the content of this book. Your guidance and wisdom were instrumental in shaping its message and ensuring its relevance to readers.

Pastor Lemuel L. Niere

A vital member of the editorial team, you worked diligently to finalize this book. Your dedication and contributions were invaluable in bringing this project to completion.

Pastor Joeveney F. Macabeo

Your unwavering support, coupled with your expertise in line editing and proofreading, provided critical assistance throughout the writing process. Your keen eye for detail and commitment to excellence elevated the quality of this book to new heights.

Sarah Green

You served as the chief editor, dedicating your expertise and insight to this project. Your extensive knowledge and exceptional talent were instrumental in ensuring the book's quality and impact.

Haley Trimmer

Your artistic talent and creativity brought both the book cover and the inside layout to life. The design you crafted captures the essence of the book, drawing readers in from the very first glance.

To each of you, I extend my deepest gratitude for your invaluable contributions, unwavering support, and dedication to excellence. This book would not have been possible without your talent, expertise, and tireless efforts. Thank you for being an integral part of this journey.

CONTENTS

FOREWORD

Every child today is born into a digital world, one that is vastly different from the world we, the parents, were born into. From as early as one or two years of age, many children are given a cell phone or tablet in place of toys to entertain themselves. For other children, the TV set becomes a babysitter. Other electronic devices, along with social media and virtual spaces, become an integral part of their lives from childhood through adolescence and young adulthood.

On the one hand, children are influenced—either positively or negatively—by what they see, hear, and observe from the actors on the screen. How can busy parents counteract the pernicious and insidious effects of media? Day after day, these seeds of worldliness are planted in the fertile imaginations of young minds. In turn, children formulate their own set of beliefs, values, and attitudes, which may undermine their personality, character, and future.

How can parents train their children to complete household tasks and school assignments conscientiously when they are so engrossed in videos and online games? How can their spirituality be enhanced? Even in church, many children continue to entertain themselves, especially when they find the sermons boring or the worship services irrelevant.

The dangers of social media to physical health include sedentary behavior and reduced sleep, while the risks to mental health include cyberbullying, exposure to pornography, missing out on face-to-face relationships, social media addiction, reduced time for other activities, and harmful postings or comments that damage online reputations and affect self-image. Additionally, social media can expose children to misleading information, scams, deceptive marketing, and content that normalizes risk-taking behaviors, such as substance abuse, suicidal ideation, hate speech, or sexual and criminal activity.

On the other hand, social media can be a tool of blessing in educational, religious, and social contexts. Among its benefits are opportunities to connect with family and friends, build relationships with peers, practice social skills, find community, and learn about or support important causes.

Children can take advantage of these benefits—but that is a big IF. Parents must know how to guide their children from an early age, helping them develop a sense of responsibility, conscientiousness, morality, and spirituality throughout their maturation process. Through this book, Pastor Jeb J. Bersabal shares foundational principles on how parents can remain connected to their children—and vice versa—in this digital world. He explains how both can remain grounded in the Christian faith as they grow together through different developmental stages and how the whole family can be guided by the Holy Spirit in this sophisticated generation.

Dr. Armand T. Fabella
Registered Psychologist / Guidance Counselor
Consultant at Gestalt Neuropsychological Services

INTRODUCTION

Welcome to "Connected, Grounded, and Guided: Parenting Spiritually in the Digital World". In this digital age, we find ourselves raising children in a world profoundly shaped by technology and connectivity.

Smartphones, tablets, laptops, and other electronic devices, along with social media and virtual spaces, have become integral components of our daily lives. They bring about both opportunities and challenges for parents and their families.

The purpose of this book is to provide guidance and insight into a crucial aspect of contemporary parenting: how to navigate the digital landscape while remaining firmly grounded in your spiritual values. As parents, we understand the significance of instilling character, values, and faith in our children. But how do we achieve this in a world where screens often mediate our interactions and influence our decisions?

In these pages, we will explore how you can remain "Connected" to your children, building strong relationships in a world where screens often mediate our interactions. We will discuss how to stay "Grounded" in your Christian values, ensuring that your family's foundation remains solid, even as the digital world continually evolves. Lastly, we will examine how you can be "Guided" by your faith, using biblical wisdom to inform your parenting choices in the digital age.

The word of God is our compass, and throughout this book, we will draw upon its teachings and stories to provide insight and guidance. Scripture will illuminate our path as we navigate topics like screen time, online safety, and digital discipleship. It will empower us to create a "Digital Covenant" for our families, a set of guidelines that reflect our Christian values and promote responsible digital citizenship.

At the heart of this book is the notion that parenting with spirituality in the digital world is not only achievable but also essential. We believe that the Christian perspective on parenting in the digital world is not just an approach but a calling. It is an opportunity to integrate your faith into your role as a parent, infusing your family's daily life with the wisdom of the word of God. Our aim is to help you nurture your child's spiritual growth, build a strong and loving family, and ultimately guide them toward a life lived in the image of Christ.

As you journey through these pages, I encourage you to reflect, pray, and seek God's guidance. This is a book for parents who wish to raise children connected to love, grounded in faith, and guided by the timeless wisdom of the word of God. I invite you to embrace the digital age with open hearts, knowing that your Christian values will be the foundation upon which your family thrives.

> **"Point your kids in the right direction— when they're old, they won't be lost."**
>
> Proverbs 22:6 - The Message (MSG)

"Your children are the greatest gift God will give to you, and their souls the heaviest responsibility He will place in your hands. Take time with them, teach them to have faith in God. Be a person in whom they can have faith. When you are old, nothing else you've done will have mattered as much."

– Lisa Wingate

"The greatest legacy one can pass on to one's children and grandchildren is not money or other material things accumulated in one's life, but rather a legacy of character and faith."

– Billy Graham

THEMES OF THE CHAPTERS

Connected, Grounded, and Guided: Parenting Spiritually in the "Digital World" offers a comprehensive guide that navigates the challenges and opportunities of nurturing children's spiritual development within an ever-evolving digital landscape.

Chapter 1 - The book delves into understanding the digital landscape, exploring both its negative impacts on parenting, such as increased screen time and cyberbullying, as well as its benefits, like access to educational resources.

Chapter 2 - Emphasizes the importance of building strong relationships in the digital age, highlighting ways to utilize digital communication tools to nurture bonds between parents and children.

Chapter 3 - Focuses on staying grounded with the Word of God amidst technological distractions, discussing strategies for balancing technology use, instilling values, and fostering resilience in children.

Chapter 4 - Explores the role of faith in guiding parenting decisions, offering insights into incorporating spirituality into daily life and using scripture to teach values to children.

Chapter 5 - Introduces the concept of digital discipleship, providing guidance on raising spiritually aware children, engaging in family devotions in a digital age, and participating in online faith communities.

Chapter 6 - Addresses common challenges such as cyberbullying, screen time management, and digital addiction, offering practical advice for parents to navigate these issues.

Chapter 7 - The book suggests creating a digital covenant within the family, setting guidelines for technology use, and finding a balance between online and offline activities.

Chapter 8 - Discusses putting faith into action and encouraging acts of compassion, kindness, and service both online and offline as part of the parenting journey.

Chapter 9 - Presents case studies illustrating spiritually grounded parenting in real-life situations, accompanied by lessons learned.

Chapter 10 - Offers insights on moving forward, emphasizing the importance of building on spiritual foundations, viewing parenting as a lifelong spiritual quest, and nurturing spiritual growth in children.

Connected, Grounded, and Guided provides a holistic approach to parenting in the digital age, combining spiritual principles with practical strategies to navigate the challenges and embrace the opportunities of raising children in today's technologically driven world.

CHAPTER I

The Digital Landscape

The digital landscape of today is a vast and ever-evolving terrain that permeates nearly every aspect of our lives. From the moment we wake up to the time we go to bed, we are surrounded by digital devices, platforms, and technologies that shape our interactions, perceptions, and experiences. In this essay, we will explore the multifaceted nature of the digital landscape, examining its impact on various facets of society and reflecting on its implications for the future.

At the heart of the digital landscape lies connectivity— the ability to access information, communicate with others, and participate in virtual communities on a global scale. The proliferation of smartphones, social media platforms, and high-speed internet has transformed the way we connect with one another, breaking down geographical barriers and facilitating instantaneous communication across continents. This unprecedented level of connectivity has revolutionized industries, from business and education to entertainment and healthcare, enabling new modes of collaboration, innovation, and engagement.

However, the digital landscape is not without its challenges and complexities. As we navigate this vast digital terrain, we are confronted with issues such as information overload, privacy concerns, and digital divides that exacerbate existing inequalities. The abundance of information available at our fingertips can be overwhelming, leading to feelings of anxiety, confusion, and cognitive overload. Moreover, the pervasive nature of digital technology has raised profound questions about privacy, security, and surveillance, prompting debates about the ethical use of data and the need for robust regulatory frameworks to protect individual rights and freedoms.

Furthermore, the digital landscape has transformed the way we consume and interact with media, blurring the lines between reality and virtuality. The rise of digital platforms such as streaming services, online gaming, and augmented reality has revolutionized entertainment and storytelling, offering immersive experiences that transcend traditional boundaries. However, this convergence of digital media has also raised concerns about the impact of excessive screen time on mental health, social relationships, and cognitive development, particularly among children and adolescents.

Despite these challenges, the digital landscape holds immense potential to drive positive change and empower individuals and communities. From the democratization of information to the amplification of marginalized voices, digital technologies have the power to foster inclusion, diversity, and social justice on a global scale.

Moreover, the rise of digital activism and online mobilization has catalyzed social movements and political change, enabling citizens to organize, protest, and advocate for their rights with unprecedented speed and efficiency.

In conclusion, the digital landscape is a complex and dynamic terrain that shapes our lives in profound ways. While it presents us with unprecedented opportunities for connection, creativity, and innovation, it also poses significant challenges that require thoughtful reflection and action. As we navigate this digital landscape, it is essential to remain vigilant, critical, and proactive in addressing the ethical, social, and political implications of digital technologies. By harnessing the transformative power of digital technology for the greater good, we can build a more inclusive, equitable, and sustainable future for generations to come.

> *"Above all else, guard your heart, for everything you do flows from it."*
>
> Proverbs 4:23 - New International Version (NIV)

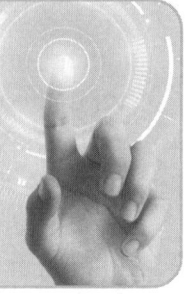

> *"The key is to teach them how to be safe with technology because ultimately, we want our children to be in charge of technology, rather than feeling technology is in charge of them."*
>
> – Elaine Halligan, London director of The Parent Practice

A. Understanding The Digital World

Understanding the digital world is the ability to comprehend and navigate the complex landscape created by modern technology and the internet. It involves not only having technical skills but also grasping the broader implications of digital technology on various aspects of life.

Here are some key points that contribute to understanding the digital world:

1. Technology Literacy: To understand the digital world, one must be literate in technology. This means having the skills and knowledge to use digital devices, software, and online services effectively. It includes knowing how to navigate the internet, use software applications, and troubleshoot common issues.

2. **Cybersecurity Awareness:** Understanding the digital world also entails being aware of cybersecurity principles. This includes knowing how to protect personal information, recognize online threats like phishing, and employ safe practices to safeguard digital assets.

3. **Digital Communication:** With the rise of digital technology, communication has evolved significantly. Understanding the digital world means being proficient in various forms of digital communication, such as email, social media, instant messaging, and video conferencing.

4. **Online Privacy:** Being aware of how personal information is collected, stored, and used online is crucial. Understanding the

digital world involves taking measures to protect one's online privacy and knowing how to adjust privacy settings on digital platforms.

5. **Economic Impact:** Digital technology has transformed the global economy. Understanding the digital world means comprehending how e-commerce, online marketplaces, and digital marketing function. It also involves recognizing the implications of automation and artificial intelligence on employment.

6. **Social and Cultural Changes:** The digital world has had a profound impact on society and culture. It has changed the way people connect, share information, and consume media. Understanding the digital world includes recognizing these social and cultural shifts.

7. **Media Literacy:** With the proliferation of online content, understanding the digital world requires media literacy. This involves the ability to critically assess information sources, identify fake news, and discern credible content from unreliable sources.

8. **Educational Opportunities:** Technology has revolutionized education. Understanding the digital world includes recognizing the potential of online learning, digital resources, and e-books in acquiring knowledge and skills.

9. **Ethical Considerations:** The digital world raises ethical questions related to issues like online behavior, digital rights, intellectual property, and the impact of technology on individuals and society. Understanding the digital world involves exploring these ethical dimensions.

10. **Adaptability and Lifelong Learning:** The digital world is in constant flux, with new technologies and trends emerging regularly. Understanding it means being adaptable and committed to lifelong learning to stay current in the ever-changing digital landscape.

In essence, understanding the digital world is about being informed, proficient, and responsible in the use of digital technology. It requires a combination of technical know-how, critical thinking, and an awareness of the societal, economic, and ethical implications of the digital age.

> *"Your word is a lamp for my feet, a light on my path."*
>
> Psalm 119:105 - New International Version (NIV)

> *"In this age of screens and pixels, let us remember to keep our hearts and minds focused on the eternal. Let us use technology not just for convenience but as a tool to spread the message of love, faith, and hope."*
>
> – Jabez Ministry

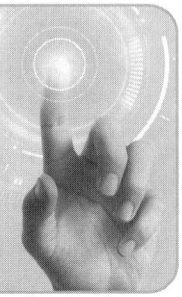

B. Negative Impact Of The Digital World On Parenting

The digital world has brought about numerous positive changes in parenting, but it has also introduced several negative impacts. Here are some of the negative effects and risk impact of the digital world on parenting:

1. **Screen Time Battles:** Excessive screen time can lead to conflicts between parents and children. Children may resist limits on their device usage, causing stress and frustration for both parents and kids.

2. **Digital Addiction:** Parents themselves may struggle with digital addiction, spending excessive time on their devices and neglecting their parenting responsibilities.

3. **Loss of Quality Time:** The constant connectivity of the digital world can lead to a loss of quality family time. Parents and children may find themselves immersed in their devices, missing out on essential face-to-face interactions.

4. **Cyberbullying:** Children may be exposed to cyberbullying, which can be emotionally distressing. Parents may struggle to address and cope with the emotional impact of cyberbullying on their children.

5. **Privacy Concerns:** Parents must navigate the challenging task of teaching their children about online privacy and security. It can be overwhelming to keep up with the latest privacy threats and educate their children effectively.

6. **Online Predators:** The digital world presents risks related to online predators. Parents may experience anxiety and fear for their children's safety online.

7. **Impact on Health:** Excessive screen time can lead to various health issues, including eye strain, sleep disturbances, and a sedentary lifestyle. Parents may need to address these health concerns in their children.

8. **Comparison and Self-Esteem:** Children may be exposed to unrealistic standards and idealized images on social media, leading to negative effects on their self-esteem. Parents may need to help their children navigate these challenges.

9. **Digital Material Exposure:** Inappropriate or harmful content can be accessed by children online. Parents must be vigilant in monitoring and filtering content to protect their children from exposure to explicit material.

10. **Influence of Technology Corporations:** Parents may feel overwhelmed by the influence of technology corporations that design apps and platforms to be addictive. These corporations may exploit children's vulnerabilities for financial gain.

11. **Interference with Parenting:** The constant distractions of digital devices can interfere with parents' ability to focus on their children. Digital notifications and the urge to check devices can disrupt meaningful interactions.

12. **Mental Health Challenges:** The digital world can contribute to mental health challenges for both parents and children. The pressure to curate a perfect online image can lead to anxiety and stress.

13. **Disconnect from Nature:** Children may become more disconnected from the natural world due to excessive screen time. Parents may need to make an effort to encourage outdoor activities and a balanced lifestyle.

14. **Poor Sleep Habits:** Exposure to screens before bedtime disrupts sleep patterns, leading to poor quality sleep for both parents and children, which can impact overall well-being and functioning.

15. **Impact on Academic Performance:** Excessive screen time can detract from academic pursuits, as it may interfere with homework completion, concentration, and overall cognitive development, ultimately affecting academic achievement.

In conclusion, the digital world has introduced a range of negative impacts on parenting, from screen time battles and digital addiction to concerns about safety, privacy, and mental health. Parents face the challenge of balancing the benefits of technology with these negative effects and risk impacts to ensure the well-being and healthy development of their children.

"Do not conform to the pattern of this world, but be transformed by the renewing of your mind."

Romans 12:2 - New International Version (NIV)

"Then you will be able to test and approve what God's will is—His good, pleasing, and perfect will. In the digital age, we have a responsibility to protect what we consider valuable and irreplaceable, which includes our children, values, and character."

– Ed Japlit

C. Benefits Of Digital World On Parenting

Here are some of the benefits of the digital world on parenting. Please note that the references provided are general and not specific to individual studies or publications:

1. **Access to Parenting Resources:** The digital world offers easy access to a vast array of parenting resources. Parents can find blogs, articles, videos, and online communities dedicated to parenting advice and tips (Common Sense Media).

2. **Educational Apps and Resources:** There are numerous educational apps and websites designed for children that provide interactive learning experiences, helping parents supplement their child's education (American Academy of Pediatrics).

3. **Communication and Connection:** Digital tools like video calls, messaging apps, and social media platforms help parents stay connected with their children, especially when separated by distance (The New York Times).

4. **Parenting Forums and Support Groups**: Online parenting forums and support groups provide a sense of community. Parents can seek advice, share experiences, and find emotional support from other parents facing similar challenges (Parents.com).

5. **Entertainment and Creativity:** The digital world offers a wide range of age-appropriate entertainment options for children, from educational games to creative apps that foster artistic and imaginative skills (HealthyChildren.org).

6. **Global Perspective:** Children can access information about different cultures and perspectives from around the world, promoting tolerance and diversity in their upbringing (UNESCO).

7. **Online Safety Tools:** Digital tools, such as parental control apps and content filters, help parents protect their children from inappropriate content and online dangers (National PTA).

8. **Learning and Skill Development:** Online resources can enhance a child's learning and skill development. For instance, coding websites can teach valuable computer programming skills (Edutopia).

9. **Digital Storytelling:** Parents can use digital platforms to create and share family stories, fostering a sense of identity and connection within the family (Psychology Today).

10. **Enhanced Access to Children's Content:** Streaming services and e-books offer a wide selection of children's content, making it convenient for parents to provide age-appropriate entertainment and educational materials (The Guardian).

As modern parents, we have found these benefits of the digital world to be valuable tools, offering support and opportunities for our children's education, communication, and overall development.

"Discipline your children, and they will give you peace; they will bring you the delights you desire."

Proverbs 29:17
- New International Version (NIV)

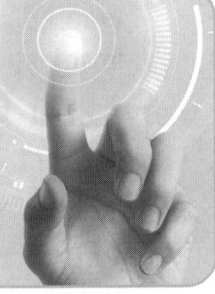

"As parents, we can use the digital world to provide our children with a safe and enriching environment for learning, exploring their faith, and deepening their understanding of God's love."

– Unknown

CHAPTER II

The Power Of Connection

In today's digital age, the power of connection between parents and children holds unparalleled significance. As parents navigating this technology-driven landscape, we recognize the crucial role that fostering strong bonds with our children plays in their overall well-being and development. Here, we delve into the importance and nuances of this connection, drawing upon our collective experiences and insights.

First and foremost, establishing a deep connection with our children amidst the pervasive nature of digital distractions provides them with a sense of emotional security and stability. In a world where screens often vie for attention, nurturing this connection serves as a steadfast anchor, offering our children a safe haven where they feel valued, understood, and unconditionally supported. This emotional security lays the groundwork for healthy self-esteem, resilience, and emotional regulation—qualities that are essential for navigating the complexities of the digital world.

Moreover, the power of connection facilitates open communication and understanding between parents and children. By prioritizing meaningful interactions and carving out dedicated time for bonding activities, we create fertile ground for fostering trust, empathy, and mutual respect within our familial relationships. These qualities, in turn, form the bedrock of effective communication, enabling us to navigate the digital landscape together as allies rather than adversaries. Through heartfelt conversations and active listening, we gain insights into our children's perspectives, concerns, and aspirations, strengthening our connection with them on both emotional and cognitive levels.

Additionally, the power of connection equips our children with invaluable resilience and coping skills necessary for thriving in the digital world. When children feel deeply connected to their parents, they are more likely to seek support during times of adversity and develop effective strategies for managing digital stressors such as cyberbullying, social media pressures, or information overload. Our unwavering support and guidance serve as a potent buffer against the negative effects of digital toxicity, empowering our children to navigate challenges with confidence and resilience.

Furthermore, our connection with our children serves as a powerful form of role modeling. By demonstrating the importance of prioritizing real-life connections over digital distractions, we impart invaluable lessons about the value of relationships and human connection in an increasingly virtual world. Through shared experiences, meaningful rituals, and quality time spent together, we cultivate a family culture that celebrates the richness of offline interactions and fosters a deep appreciation for the joys of genuine human connection.

In conclusion, the power of connection between parents and children in the digital world is not merely a luxury but a necessity. As parents committed to nurturing strong bonds with our children, we recognize the transformative impact that genuine connection can have on their emotional well-being, personal development, and resilience in the face of digital challenges. By prioritizing meaningful interactions, open communication, and unconditional love, we pave the way for our children to thrive in both the digital realm and the vast terrain of human relationships.

> *"Love the Lord your God with all your heart, all your soul, and all your strength. Always remember these commands I give you today. Teach them to your children and talk about them when you sit at home and walk along the road, when you lie down and when you get up. Write them down and tie them to your hands as a sign. Tie them on your forehead to remind you."*
>
> Deuteronomy 6:5-8 - New Century Version (NCV)

> *"With our connection to God, we are always in touch with the solutions we are seeking."*
>
> – Wayne Dyer & Ed Japlit

A. Building Strong Relationships

Building strong relationships between parents and children is crucial for healthy family dynamics. Here are ten strategies that we, as parents, can implement to strengthen these bonds:

1. **Open Communication**: We prioritize open and honest communication with our children, creating a safe space for them to express their thoughts, feelings, and concerns without fear of judgment or criticism (Ponciano et al., 2019).

2. **Quality Time Together**: We make a conscious effort to spend quality time with our children, engaging in activities that they enjoy and showing genuine interest in their lives (Blair & Umberson, 2017).

3. **Active Listening:** We actively listen to our children, giving them our full attention and validating their experiences, which helps to foster trust and understanding (McLeod, 2017).

4. **Setting Boundaries with Respect:** We set clear and consistent boundaries with our children, ensuring that they understand the rules and consequences while also respecting their autonomy and individuality (Simons & Conger, 2007).

5. **Positive Reinforcement:** We use positive reinforcement to acknowledge and encourage our children's efforts and achievements, boosting their self-esteem and motivation (Gershoff, 2013).

6. **Empathy and Understanding:** We strive to empathize with our children's perspectives and experiences, showing understanding and compassion even during challenging situations (Eisenberg et al., 2016).

7. **Leading by Example:** We model positive behaviors and values for our children, demonstrating respect, empathy, and resilience in our own actions and interactions (Bandura, 1977).

8. **Quality Family Rituals:** We establish meaningful family rituals and traditions, such as weekly game nights or holiday celebrations, to strengthen our family bonds and create lasting memories (Fiese et al., 2002).

9. **Conflict Resolution Skills:** We teach our children healthy conflict resolution skills, emphasizing the importance of listening, compromise, and finding mutually beneficial solutions (Katz & Gottman, 1996).

10. **Unconditional Love and Support:** Above all, we show our children unconditional love and support, reassuring them that they are valued and cherished members of our family, no matter what (Rohner, 2004).

By implementing these strategies, we can nurture strong and resilient relationships with our children, laying the foundation for their emotional well-being and future success.

"My child, when the Lord corrects you, pay close attention and take it as a warning. The Lord corrects those He loves, as parents correct a child of whom they are proud."

Proverbs 3:11-12
- Good News Translation (GNT)

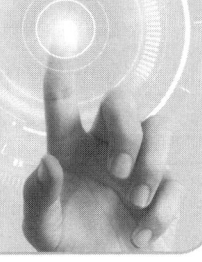

> *"Our children need to feel love, not condemnation. They should trust that we're an ally, not the enemy. You're not fighting against your kids in hopes of coming out victorious over them; you're in a battle for them."*
>
> – O'Dell

B. Digital Communication With Our Children

1. **Video Calls:** Utilizing video calling platforms such as Zoom, Skype, or FaceTime allowsfor face-to-face communication with our children, even when we're physically apart. Theseplatforms enable us to see each other's expressions, share experiences, and maintain a senseof closeness despite the distance.

2. **Messaging Apps:** Messaging apps like WhatsApp, Messenger, or iMessage provide convenient ways to stay in touch with our children throughout the day. Whether sending quick updates, sharing photos, or having casual conversations, these apps offer instant communication and help foster a sense of connection.

3. **Email:** Email remains a reliable means of digital communication, especially for longer ormore formal conversations. Encouraging our children to use email for school-related matters, sharing stories, or expressing thoughts can help them develop valuable writing skills while keeping us connected.

4. **Social Media:** While social media comes with its risks, using platforms like Instagram, Twitter, or Facebook can be beneficial for staying connected with older children. Following each other's accounts, sharing posts, and engaging in meaningful conversations online can strengthen our bond and provide insights into each other's lives.

5. **Online Games:** Playing online games together can be a fun and interactive way to communicate with our children, especially teenagers. Whether it's collaborating on multiplayer games,

competing in trivia challenges, or simply chatting while playing, gaming provides opportunities for shared experiences and bonding.

6. **Shared Calendars:** Digital calendar apps like Google Calendar or Apple Calendar allow families to coordinate schedules, plan activities, and stay organized together. Sharing calendars ensures everyone is on the same page regarding appointments, events, and commitments, facilitating effective communication and time management.

7. **Parental Control Apps:** While not a direct communication tool, parental control apps like Qustodio, Bark, or Family Link can help monitor and manage our children's digital activities. By setting healthy boundaries, enforcing screen time limits, and promoting responsible online behavior, these apps facilitate constructive communication and ensure a safer digital experience for our children.

8. **Online Learning Platforms:** Explore online learning platforms such as Khan Academy, Coursera, or Duolingo as avenues for interactive learning and skill-building with your children. Choose topics of mutual interest, such as coding, language learning, or science experiments, and embark on learning journeys together. This shared pursuit of knowledge promotes intellectual curiosity, fosters a growth mindset, and strengthens your connection through shared learning experiences.

> *"When you speak to people, always speak kind words. Say things that will help them. Then, when someone asks you a question, you will know how to reply."*
>
> Colossians 4:6
> – Easy English Bible (EASY)

> *"Research shows that parenting with rules and boundaries but with love and caring promotes better everything: better grades in school, better relationships with their friends and family, everything!"*
>
> – Ruston

C. Nurturing Bonds Through Technology

As Christian parents, nurturing bonds through technology involves more than simply using digital tools. It entails leveraging these tools to strengthen our relationships with our loved ones, particularly our children, and to deepen our faith together. Here are ten ways we can utilize technology to enhance relationships and cultivate deeper connections between parents and children:

1. **Virtual Family Bible Study:** We gather as a family for virtual Bible study sessions using video conferencing platforms like Zoom or Google Meet. Together, we select a passage or topic to study, share our insights, and pray for each other's spiritual growth.

2. **Online Worship Services:** We attend online worship services together as a family, streaming live church services or watching recorded sermons. Participating in worship and listening to God's word as a family helps us grow closer to each other and to God.

3. **Family Devotionals:** Using devotion apps or websites, we incorporate daily family devotionals into our routine. These devotionals include scripture readings, reflections, and prayers that we discuss together and apply to our lives.

4. **Digital Prayer Chain:** We create a digital prayer chain using messaging apps or social media groups. Each family member shares prayer requests, and we commit to praying for each other's needs regularly, fostering unity and support in prayer.

5. **Virtual Mission Projects:** We engage in virtual mission projects as a family, such as supporting missionary organizations or participating in online outreach programs. Through digital platforms, we contribute to spreading the love of Christ and serving others in need.

6. **Christian Podcasts or Audiobooks:** We listen to Christian podcasts or audiobooks together as a family, discussing the messages and insights shared. This activity nurtures our bonds and deepens our understanding of biblical principles and Christian living.

7. **Online Christian Courses or Webinars:** We enroll in online Christian courses or webinars together, exploring topics like theology, discipleship, or spiritual growth. Engaging in learning opportunities as a family strengthens our knowledge and faith while fostering meaningful discussions.

8. **Digital Worship Journals:** Each family member maintains a digital worship journal using note-taking apps or journaling platforms. We write down prayers, reflections, and gratitude lists, sharing our experiences and spiritual journeys with one another.

9. **Virtual Fellowship with Other Believers:** We connect with other Christian families for virtual fellowship and mutual encouragement. Hosting online prayer meetings, Bible studies, or Christian book clubs allows us to build relationships with fellow believers and grow together in faith.

10. **Sharing Christian Content:** We share uplifting Christian content, such as inspirational quotes, devotional readings, or worship songs, with each other through messaging apps or social media platforms. By spreading messages of hope and encouragement, we reinforce our bonds and strengthen our faith as a family.

By embracing technology as a tool for connection and communication, we can cultivate strong and meaningful relationships with our children while growing closer to God and fostering love, support, and understanding in today's digital world.

"And now a word to you parents. Don't keep on scolding and nagging your children, making them angry and resentful. Rather, bring them up with the loving discipline the Lord Himself approves, with suggestions and godly advice."

Ephesians 6:4 - Living Bible (TLB)

"Many parents fear that if they approach certain topics too early, it will give their kids ideas about those things before they actually need to face them. Let me ask you some questions…Do your kids ride the school bus with older kids? Are there older kids in your neighborhood? …You may shield your tweens from talk of dating and teen relationships, but what about the eleventh graders making out in the back of the bus? You might supervise Internet activity, but what about the computers at friends' houses?"

– Nicole O'Dell, author of Hot Button Topics: Internet Edition

CHAPTER III

Grounded With The Word Of God

In today's digital age, where screens and devices dominate our daily lives, the importance of being grounded in the Word of God remains paramount, especially in the realm of parenting. Amidst the constant barrage of digital distractions and ever-evolving technological landscapes, grounding ourselves and our children in the timeless truths of Scripture is essential for nurturing faith, character, and healthy relationships. This essay explores the significance of being grounded with the Word of God in the digital world, focusing particularly on its importance in parenting.

Firstly, being grounded in the Word of God provides a solid foundation for parenting amidst the digital onslaught. The rapid advancement of technology has ushered in unprecedented challenges for us as parents, from managing screen time to navigating online risks and influences. In this digital milieu, the principles and values found in Scripture serve as guiding beacons, offering timeless wisdom on raising children in a technology-saturated society. Proverbs 22:6 admonishes, *"Train up a child in the way he should go; even when he is old, he will not depart from it,"* emphasizing the importance of instilling godly values and principles from a young age. By grounding our parenting practices in the Word of God, we can navigate the complexities of the digital world with confidence and discernment, ensuring that our children grow up with a strong moral compass and spiritual foundation.

Furthermore, being grounded in the Word of God fosters meaningful engagement and discipleship in the digital realm. The pervasive influence of digital media presents both opportunities and challenges for us as parents seeking to nurture our children's faith and character. While screens can be used as tools for learning and connection, they also expose children to a myriad of messages and ideologies that may contradict biblical truth. In this context, grounding our children in the Word of God equips them to discern between what is true and false, noble and base, even in the digital sphere. Deuteronomy 6:6-7 instructs parents, *"These commandments that I give you today are to be on your hearts. Impress them on your children. Talk about them when you sit at home and when you walk along the road, when you lie down and when you get up,"* highlighting the importance of consistent and intentional discipleship within the family. By incorporating biblical principles into everyday conversations and interactions, we can help our children develop a biblical worldview that permeates every aspect of their lives, including their digital habits and interactions.

Moreover, being grounded in the Word of God cultivates resilience and spiritual vitality in the face of digital pressures and temptations. The digital world, with its instant gratification and constant connectivity, can exert significant pressure on children and parents alike, leading to anxiety, comparison, and spiritual apathy. However, Psalm 119:11 reminds us, *"I have hidden your word in my heart that I might not sin against you,"* affirming the transformative power of Scripture in guarding our hearts and minds against the allure of worldly distractions. By grounding ourselves and our children in the Word of God, we can nurture resilience, faith, and spiritual vitality that withstand the challenges of the digital age. This involves not only setting boundaries and guidelines for digital use but also cultivating a deep love for God's Word and a vibrant relationship with Him that transcends the digital realm.

In conclusion, being grounded in the Word of God is indispensable for parenting in the digital world. By anchoring ourselves and our children in the timeless truths and principles of Scripture, we can navigate the complexities of the digital age with wisdom, discernment, and grace. As we model and teach our children to love and obey God's Word, we can raise a generation that remains steadfast in faith, resilient in character, and grounded in the unchanging love of Christ, both online and offline.

> "The whole Bible was given to us by inspiration from God and is useful to teach us what is true and to make us realize what is wrong in our lives; it straightens us out and helps us do what is right. It is God's way of making us well prepared at every point, fully equipped to do good to everyone."
>
> 2 Timothy 3:16-17 - Living Bible (TLB)

> "Bible study is especially needed in the schools. Students should be rooted and grounded in divine truth; their attention should be called not to the assertions of men but to the word of God. Above all other books, the word of God must be our study, the great textbook, the basis of all education, and our children are to be educated in the truths found therein, irrespective of previous habits and customs."
>
> – Testimonies for the church volume 6, p. 131, 132

A. Balancing Technology Use

In our Christian approach to parenting, balancing technology use is a significant aspect of nurturing our children in a manner that aligns with biblical principles and values. While technology offers numerous benefits and opportunities for learning, connection, and entertainment, it also presents challenges and potential pitfalls that can impact our children's spiritual, emotional, and social development. Therefore, we strive to find a balanced approach to technology use that fosters healthy growth and honors God in all aspects of life.

1. **Setting Boundaries:** We recognize the importance of setting boundaries around technology use to ensure that it remains a tool for positive purposes rather than a source of harm. This may involve establishing limits on screen time, regulating access to certain types of content, and creating technology-free zones or times within our homes. By setting clear boundaries, we can help our children develop self-discipline, prioritize healthy activities, and maintain a balanced lifestyle.

2. **Modeling Healthy Habits:** Children learn by example, so we seek to model healthy technology habits in our own lives. This includes demonstrating moderation in our own use of devices, prioritizing face-to-face interactions over digital communication, and engaging in activities that foster spiritual growth and family bonding. By modeling balanced technology use, we can instill values of self-control, mindfulness, and stewardship of time and resources in our children.

3. **Teaching Discernment:** In a digital world filled with diverse messages and influences, we play a crucial role in teaching our children discernment. This involves helping them critically evaluate the content they encounter online, discerning between truth and falsehood, and understanding how their choices in digital media can impact their beliefs, attitudes, and behaviors. By grounding our children in the truth of God's Word, we empower them to make wise choices and stand firm in their faith amidst the complexities of the digital age.

4. **Emphasizing Relationships:** We prioritize nurturing meaningful relationships within our families and communities over excessive reliance on technology for social interaction. We encourage open communication, quality time spent together, and opportunities for genuine connection that transcend virtual interactions. By fostering strong relationships rooted in love, trust, and mutual respect, we create a supportive environment where our children

feel valued, understood, and affirmed, reducing the temptation to seek validation or fulfillment solely through digital means.

5. **Cultivating Spiritual Growth:** Ultimately, we view technology as a tool to support, rather than supplant, our efforts to nurture our children's spiritual growth. We integrate technology into family devotional times, Bible study sessions, and other spiritual practices in ways that enhance engagement and understanding of God's Word. By harnessing technology for edifying purposes, we can foster a deepening of our children's relationship with God, encouraging them to seek His guidance and wisdom in all areas of life.

In summary, our Christian approach to balancing technology use in parenting involves setting boundaries, modeling healthy habits, teaching discernment, emphasizing relationships, and cultivating spiritual growth. By adopting a holistic approach that integrates biblical principles with practical strategies for navigating the digital world, we seek to equip our children to use technology responsibly, discerningly, and in a manner that glorifies God.

> *"Keep your minds thinking about things in heaven. Do not think about things on the earth."*
>
> Colossians 3:2 - New Life Version (NLV)

"This verse encourages us to prioritize spiritual matters over worldly pursuits. While technology can be useful and enjoyable, we should not allow it to distract us from our relationship with God or our responsibilities as believers, especially in regard to our children."

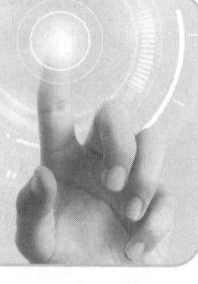

B. Values And Ethics In A Digital World

As Christian parents, we recognize the profound impact of values and ethics in navigating the complexities of the digital world. In today's technologically driven society, where information is readily accessible and online interactions are pervasive, instilling biblical values and ethical principles in our children is paramount.

First and foremost, we understand that our values are rooted in God's Word. The Bible serves as our ultimate guide for discerning right from wrong, truth from falsehood, and righteousness from unrighteousness. Therefore, we prioritize the study and application of Scripture in our parenting journey, teaching our children to align their beliefs and behaviors with the teachings of Jesus Christ.

In the digital realm, where moral boundaries are often blurred, and ethical dilemmas abound, we strive to model integrity and righteousness in our online interactions. Whether it's through social media, online gaming, or browsing the internet, we emphasize the importance of honesty, kindness, and respect towards others. We teach our children to use technology responsibly, understanding that every digital action has real-world consequences and impacts not only themselves but also those around them.

Moreover, we actively engage in conversations with our children about the ethical implications of their online activities. We discuss topics such as cyberbullying, privacy concerns, and digital citizenship, empowering them to make informed decisions and exercise discernment in their online behavior. We encourage critical thinking and moral reasoning, equipping our children to navigate ethical dilemmas with wisdom and grace.

At the heart of our approach to parenting in the digital age is the cultivation of a Christ-centered worldview. We teach our children to view technology as a tool for glorifying God and serving others, rather than as a means of self-indulgence or gratification. We encourage them to use their digital platforms and talents to spread love, share the gospel, and make a positive impact in the world.

In summary, the Christian approach to parenting in the digital age revolves around instilling biblical values, modeling ethical behavior, fostering open communication, and cultivating a Christ-centered worldview. By grounding our children in the truth of God's Word and equipping them with moral discernment, we empower them to navigate the digital world with integrity, compassion, and purpose.

> *"'I have the right to do anything,' you say—but not everything is beneficial. 'I have the right to do anything'—but I will not be mastered by anything."*
>
> 1 Corinthians 6:12
> – New International Version (NIV)

"This verse emphasizes the importance of moderation and self-control in all aspects of life, including the use of technology. While technology offers many benefits, it should not become a master over us."

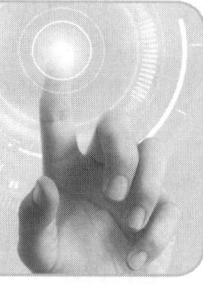

C. Fostering Resilience

As parents, fostering resilience in our children is a cornerstone of our parenting approach. In a world filled with challenges, trials, and uncertainties, we recognize the importance of equipping our children with the inner strength, faith, and perseverance needed to overcome obstacles and thrive in every circumstance. Here are ten Christian approaches to parenting that we employ in fostering resilience in our children:

1. **Grounding in Faith:** We prioritize nurturing a strong foundation of faith in our children,teaching them to trust in God's sovereignty, goodness, and faithfulness. By grounding themin biblical truths and fostering a personal relationship with Jesus Christ, we instill in them a source of unwavering strength and hope amidst life's challenges.

2. **Modeling Resilience:** We lead by example, demonstrating resilience in our own lives as we navigate difficulties and setbacks. Through our attitudes, actions, and responses to adversity, we show our children the importance of perseverance, resilience, and trust in God's provision.

3. **Encouraging Perseverance:** We encourage our children to persevere in the face of obstacles, setbacks, and failures. Rather than avoiding challenges or giving up easily, we teach them the value of resilience and determination in achieving their goals and fulfillingGod's purposes for their lives.

4. **Fostering a Growth Mindset:** We cultivate a growth mindset in our children, emphasizing the belief that their abilities and intelligence can be developed through effort, perseverance, and learning from mistakes. By fostering a positive attitude towards challenges and failures, we empower our children to embrace setbacks as opportunities for growth and improvement.

5. **Building Self-Efficacy:** We help our children develop a sense of self-efficacy – the beliefin their own abilities to overcome obstacles and achieve success. Through encouragement, affirmation, and support, we nurture their confidence and resilience, enabling them to facechallenges with courage and determination.

6. **Providing Supportive Relationships:** We cultivate a supportive family environment where our children feel loved, accepted, and valued unconditionally. By fostering strong, nurturing relationships

within the family and community, we provide our children with a secure foundation from which to explore, grow, and thrive.

7. **Teaching Coping Skills:** We equip our children with practical coping skills to manage stress, anxiety, and adversity. Through teaching techniques such as problem-solving, emotional regulation, and positive self-talk, we empower our children to navigate life's challenges with resilience and grace.

8. **Cultivating Gratitude:** We foster an attitude of gratitude in our children, teaching them to recognize and appreciate God's blessings, even in difficult circumstances. By cultivating a thankful heart, we help our children maintain perspective, resilience, and joy amidst trials and tribulations.

9. **Encouraging Faith Community:** We encourage our children to connect with a supportive faith community where they can find encouragement, fellowship, and spiritual nourishment. By participating in church activities, youth groups, and service opportunities, our children develop relationships and support networks that reinforce their faith and resilience.

10. **Practicing Prayer and Trust:** Above all, we teach our children the power of prayer and trust in God's providence. Through regular prayer, we invite God into every aspect of our lives, seeking His guidance, strength, and comfort. By entrusting our cares and concerns to Him, we cultivate a deep sense of peace, resilience, and dependence on God's unfailing love and grace.

In summary, fostering resilience in our children involves grounding them in faith, modeling resilience, encouraging perseverance, fostering a growth mindset, building self-efficacy, providing supportive relationships, teaching coping skills, cultivating gratitude, encouraging participation in the faith community, and practicing prayer and trust in God. By embracing these Christian approaches to parenting, we equip our children with the tools, values, and faith needed to navigate life's challenges with resilience, courage, and grace.

"We can rejoice, too, when we run into problems and trials, for we know that they are good for us—they help us learn to be patient. And patience develops strength of character in us and helps us trust God more each time we use it until finally our hope and faith are strong and steady. Then, when that happens, we are able to hold our heads high no matter what happens and know that all is well, for we know how dearly God loves us, and we feel this warm love everywhere within us because God has given us the Holy Spirit to fill our hearts with His love."

Romans 5:3-5 - Living Bible (TLB)

"Resilience is our ability to bounce back from life's challengesand unforeseen difficulties, providing mental protection from emotional and mental disorders."

– Michael Rutter (1985)

CHAPTER IV

Guiding With Faith

In navigating the complexities of parenting in the digital age, Christians are called to uphold certain principles rooted in their faith. The Bible serves as our guidebook, offering timeless wisdom applicable to contemporary challenges. As we embark on the journey of nurturing our children in a digital world, we are tasked with the responsibility of guiding them with faith, anchoring our approach in biblical foundations.

First and foremost, Proverbs 22:6 admonishes us to, *"Train up a child in the way he should go, and when he is old, he will not depart from it."* This verse underscores the importance of intentional and consistent guidance from an early age. In the context of digital parenting, it emphasizes the significance of instilling values such as discernment, responsibility, and self-control in our children's interactions with technology.

The Apostle Paul's exhortation in Ephesians 6:4 provides further insight, urging parents not to provoke their children to anger but to bring them up in the discipline and instruction of the Lord. This verse reminds us of the delicate balance between authority and compassion, discipline and grace. Applying this principle to the digital realm necessitates open communication, mutual respect, and the cultivation of a trusting relationship where children feel comfortable seeking guidance and accountability.

Philippians 4:8 offers a blueprint for discerning what is beneficial in a world inundated with digital stimuli: *"Finally, brothers and sisters, whatever is true, whatever is noble, whatever is right, whatever is pure, whatever is lovely, whatever is admirable—if anything is excellent or praiseworthy—think about such things."*

As parents, we are called to guide our children in discerning between that which uplifts and edifies their minds and spirits and that which leads to harm or distraction.

In light of these biblical principles, a Christian approach to parenting in the digital world involves proactive engagement rather than reactive restriction. Instead of merely imposing rules and limitations, we seek to cultivate a deep understanding of the underlying values and principles that govern our choices. We strive to model healthy digital habits ourselves, recognizing that our actions often speak louder than words.

Central to our approach is the cultivation of spiritual resilience. Just as we equip our children with physical armor to protect them from harm, we also provide them with spiritual armor, as outlined in Ephesians 6:10-18. Through prayer, Scripture reading, and fellowship with other believers, we fortify their hearts and minds against the onslaught of negative influences prevalent in the digital sphere.

Furthermore, we recognize the importance of teaching discernment in the digital age. In Ephesians 5:15-16, we are urged to be wise and careful in how we live, making the most of every opportunity because the days are evil. Similarly, in James 1:5, we are encouraged to ask God for wisdom, knowing that He gives generously to all without finding fault. Guided by these principles, we help our children develop critical thinking skills and discernment, enabling them to navigate the digital world with wisdom, discretion, and moral integrity.

Moreover, we embrace technology as a tool for advancing God's kingdom and fulfilling our mission as disciples of Christ. Whether through online ministry, virtual community engagement, or creative expression, we encourage our children to harness the power of technology for positive purposes, thereby redeeming what has been corrupted by sin.

Additionally, we comprehend the importance of safeguarding our children's hearts and minds in the digital age. Proverbs 4:23 serves as a reminder to prioritize guarding our hearts above all else, recognizing that all our actions flow from it. Hence, we remain vigilant in monitoring our children's online activities, shielding them from detrimental content and influences, and steering them towards that which is true, noble, right, pure, lovely, and admirable (Philippians 4:8). Through protecting their hearts and minds, we aid in nurturing a robust moral compass and discerning spirit that will serve as guiding lights throughout their lives.

In conclusion, guiding with faith in the digital world entails anchoring our parenting approach in biblical principles such as intentional training, loving discipline, discerning wisdom, and spiritual resilience. By embodying these values and modeling Christ-like behavior, we equip our children to navigate the complexities of the digital age with wisdom, integrity, and grace. As we entrust them into God's care, we rest assured that He who began a good work in them will carry it on to completion (Philippians 1:6), even amidst the challenges of the digital era.

"Don't worry about anything; instead, pray about everything; tell God your needs, and don't forget to thank Him for His answers. If you do this, you will experience God's peace, which is far more wonderful than the human mind can understand. His peace will keep your thoughts and your hearts quiet and at rest as you trust in Christ Jesus."

Philippians 4:6-7 - Living Bible (TLB)

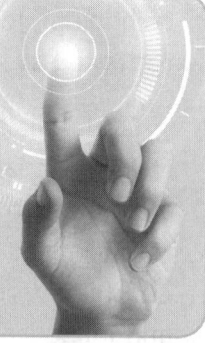

"No matter what has happened to you in the past or what is going on in your life right now, it has no power to keep you from having an amazingly good future if you walk by faith in God. God loves you! He wants you to live with victory over sin so you can possess His promises for your life today!"

– Joyce Meyer

A. The Role Of Spirituality

As parents, prioritizing spirituality entails deliberately cultivating a vibrant relationship with God within our families. We incorporate spiritual practices such as prayer, Bible study, and worship into our daily routines, both offline and online. We actively encourage our children to develop a personal connection with God, guiding them to seek His guidance and wisdom in all aspects of their lives, including their digital interactions.

Here are 10 Christ-like method principles concerning the role of spirituality in parenting in the digital world, along with their corresponding references:

1. **Prioritizing Prayer and Reflection:** We prioritize regular prayer and reflection as a family, seeking God's guidance and wisdom in navigating the digital world. (Philippians 4:6-7)

2. **Modeling Christ-like Behavior:** We model Christ-like behavior in our digital interactions, demonstrating virtues such as love, kindness, and patience. (Ephesians 5:1-2)

3. **Encouraging Scripture Study:** We encourage the study of Scripture as a family, seeking to understand and apply God's Word to our digital lives. (2 Timothy 3:16-17)

4. **Fostering a Spirit of Gratitude:** We cultivate a spirit of gratitude within our family, recognizing and thanking God for the blessings and opportunities afforded to us in the digital world. (1 Thessalonians 5:16-18)

5. **Emphasizing the Power of Forgiveness:** We emphasize the importance of forgiveness and reconciliation in our digital interactions, following Christ's example of extending grace and mercy to others. (Ephesians 4:32)

6. **Promoting Humility and Servanthood:** We promote humility and servanthood in our online interactions, seeking to serve others with humility and grace. (Philippians 2:3-4)

7. **Cultivating a Heart of Compassion:** We cultivate a heart of compassion for those we encounter online, seeking to show Christ's love and compassion to all. (Colossians 3:12)

8. **Practicing Discernment and Wisdom:** We practice discernment and wisdom in our digital activities, seeking God's guidance and discernment to navigate the complexities of the online world. (James 1:5)

9. **Building Authentic Relationships:** We prioritize building authentic relationships online, seeking to connect with others in meaningful and genuine ways. (1 John 4:7)

10. **Remaining Steadfast in Faith:** We remain steadfast in our faith amidst the challenges of the digital world, trusting in God's provision and guidance in all circumstances. (Hebrews 10:23)

These Christ-like method principles serve as foundational guidelines for parenting in the digital world, guiding us to embody the character of Christ in all our interactions and activities online.

> *"Training your body helps you in some ways. But devotion to God helps you in every way. It brings you blessings in this life and in the future life, too."*
>
> 1 Timothy 4:8 - Easy-to-Read Version (ERV)

> *"Jesus tells His followers to seek first God's kingdom, 'and all these things will be added to you.'*
> *We are to trust and obey God and follow His call in every inch of our lives, in every second of our time, and with every gift with which we have been endowed. And we are then to leave the result as well as the assessment to God."*
>
> – Os Guinness, Renaissance

B. Incorporating Faith Into Daily Life

As parents navigating the digital world, we are tasked with teaching our children how to incorporate faith into their daily lives amidst the myriad of digital distractions and influences. Drawing from biblical teaching, here's how we, as a family, approach this important endeavor:

1. **Modeling Faithfulness:** We understand the significance of modeling faithfulness to our children, both online and offline. By living out our faith authentically in the digital sphere, we demonstrate to our children how to prioritize God in all aspects of life. Our consistent example serves as a powerful testimony of God's presence and relevance in the digital world. (Matthew 5:16) Our actions speak louder than words, and our children learn by observing how we navigate challenges, express gratitude, and prioritize our relationship with God.

2. **Encouraging Digital Devotion:** We integrate digital devotionals, podcasts, and online Bible studies into our family's routine, encouraging our children to engage with faith-based content on digital platforms. By providing them with access to uplifting and edifying resources, we help them cultivate a habit of seeking God in the midst of their online activities. (Psalm 119:11). Through guided study, we help our children understand the foundational truths of our faith and how they can apply them in their daily routines.

3. **Practicing Prayer and Reflection:** We teach our children the importance of digital prayer and reflection, showing them that they can connect with God anytime and anywhere, even through their digital devices. We encourage them to take moments throughout their day to pause, pray, and reflect on God's presence and guidance in their lives, fostering a sense of spiritual awareness in the digital realm. (Philippians 4:6-7). By fostering a habit of prayer and reflection, we help our children recognize God's presence and guidance in their lives.

4. **Discernment in Digital Engagement:** We equip our children with discernment skills to navigate the digital world wisely, helping them distinguish between content that aligns with their faith and that which does not. Through open dialogue and guidance grounded in biblical principles, we empower them to make thoughtful choices about their digital consumption, ensuring that their online interactions reflect their values and beliefs. (Proverbs 4:23). As parents, our role is to guide and support our children as they develop the discernment, they need to honor God in all aspects of their lives, including their digital engagement.

5. **Fostering Digital Community:** We prioritize involvement in digital communities that promote faith and spiritual growth, such as online youth groups or Christian forums. By connecting with like-minded peers and mentors in the digital space, our children have the opportunity to build supportive relationships, share their faith journey, and encourage one another in their walk with God. (Hebrews 10:24-25). We encourage our children to participate in church activities, youth groups, and other gatherings where they can build relationships with other believers and grow in their faith together.

6. **Integrating Faith into Digital Practices:** As parents, we encourage our children to incorporate faith into their digital practices, whether it's sharing encouraging messages on social media, participating in online prayer groups, or using digital platforms to support charitable causes. By infusing their digital activities with faith, they can be a light for Christ in the digital world, spreading His love and truth to others (Colossians 3:17). Additionally, we can assist our children by promoting values of kindness, respect, and compassion in their digital interactions, guiding them to become positive influences in their online communities.

7. **Emphasizing Digital Stewardship:** We emphasize the importance of digital stewardship, teaching our children to use their online platforms and resources responsibly and ethically. By promoting values of integrity, warm- warm-heartedness, and dignity

in their digital interactions, they can reflect the character of Christ and positively impact their digital communities (1 Corinthians 10:31). Just as we teach them to discern right from wrong in the physical world, we empower them to apply the same principles to their online activities. In emphasizing digital stewardship, we encourage them to critically evaluate the content they consume and share, considering whether it aligns with their faith and value

By implementing these biblical principles into our parenting approach in the digital world, we aim to equip our children with the tools and foundation they need to live out their faith daily, both online and offline. Our ultimate goal is to raise children who are grounded in their relationship with God and who shine His light brightly in the digital sphere.

"But he's already made it plain how to live, what to do, what God is looking for in men and women.

It's quite simple: Do what is fair and just to your neighbor, be compassionate and loyal in your love,

And don't take yourself too seriously
— take God seriously."

Micah 6:8 - The Message (MSG)

"Faith is not a once-in-a-while thing; it's an all-the-time thing. It's about trusting God in the big decisions and the small moments of everyday life."

– Max Lucado

C. Using Scripture To Teach Values

In the digital age, where screens and devices are ubiquitous, the importance of using Scripture to teach the values of God cannot be overstated, especially in the realm of parenting. As parents navigating the complexities of raising children in a technology-driven world, we recognize the profound impact that digital media can have on our children's beliefs, attitudes, and behaviors. Therefore, we strive to integrate the timeless truths of Scripture into our parenting approach, guiding our children to discern God's values amidst the digital noise.

Firstly, using Scripture to teach the values of God provides a solid foundation for parenting in the digital world. Just as the psalmist declares, *"Your word is a lamp for my feet, a light on my path"* (Psalm 119:105), we believe that God's Word illuminates the path of parenting, offering timeless wisdom and guidance. In a digital landscape filled with conflicting messages and influences, grounding our parenting practices in Scripture equips us to navigate the complexities with discernment and confidence. By teaching our children the values of God found in Scripture, such as love, kindness, and integrity, we provide them with a moral compass to navigate the digital world with grace and wisdom.

Furthermore, using Scripture to teach the values of God fosters meaningful engagement and discipleship in the digital realm. The pervasive influence of digital media presents both opportunities and challenges for parents seeking to nurture their children's faith. However, as the apostle Paul instructs, *"Do not conform to the pattern of this world, but be transformed by the renewing of your mind"* (Romans 12:2), we recognize the importance of shaping our children's minds and hearts according to God's Word, rather than the values of the digital culture. By incorporating Scripture into our digital interactions and discussions, we create opportunities for our children to grow in their understanding of God's values and apply them to their online behaviors.

Moreover, using Scripture to teach the values of God cultivates resilience and spiritual vitality in the face of digital pressures and temptations. The digital world, with its constant connectivity and instant gratification, can exert significant pressure on children and parents alike. However, as the psalmist declares, *"I have hidden your word in my heart that I might not sin against you"* (Psalm 119:11), we believe that Scripture serves as a powerful tool for guarding our hearts and minds against the allure of worldly distractions. By grounding our children in the truth of God's Word, we empower them to resist temptation, overcome challenges, and thrive spiritually in the digital age.

In conclusion, using Scripture to teach the values of God is indispensable for parenting in the digital world. By anchoring ourselves and our children in the timeless truths and principles of Scripture, we equip them to navigate the complexities of the digital age with wisdom, discernment, and grace. As we model and teach our children to love and obey God's Word, we raise a generation that remains steadfast and connected in faith, resilient and guided by the character of Christ, and grounded in the unchanging love of Christ, both online and offline.

"For the word of God is alive and active. Sharper than any double-edged sword, it penetrates even to dividing soul and spirit, joints and marrow; it judges the thoughts and attitudes of the heart."

Hebrews 4:12 - New International Version (NIV)

"In a world full of conflicting messages, teaching children the unchanging truths of Scripture provides them with a moral anchor that will steady them in the storms of life."

– Unknown

CHAPTER V

Digital Discipleship

In the modern era, the concept of discipleship has taken on new dimensions with the advent of digital technology. Digital discipleship refers to the practice of using digital platforms and tools to spread the teachings of Christ, connect with fellow believers, and nurture spiritual growth. As parents navigating the complexities of raising children in the digital age, we recognize the profound importance of digital discipleship in shaping our children's faith and character.

Digital discipleship offers unprecedented opportunities for parents to engage their children in meaningful conversations about faith. Just as Jesus instructed His disciples to go and make disciples of all nations (Matthew 28:19), we are called to impart the teachings of Christ to our children and disciple them in the ways of the Lord. In the digital realm, this involves leveraging online resources such as Bible apps, devotionals, and Christian websites to facilitate discussions about Scripture, prayer, and Christian living. By integrating digital discipleship into our parenting approach, we create opportunities for our children to grow in their understanding of God's Word and develop a personal relationship with Jesus Christ.

Digital discipleship enables parents to connect their children with a global community of believers. As the apostle Paul writes, *"Encourage one another and build each other up"* (1 Thessalonians 5:11), we recognize the importance of surrounding our children with a supportive Christian community that spans geographical boundaries. Through online platforms such as social media, forums, and virtual church services, we can expose our children to diverse perspectives, testimonies, and expressions of faith. By fostering connections with fellow believers from around the world, we expand our children's understanding of the Body of Christ and cultivate a sense of belonging within the larger Christian community.

Digital discipleship empowers parents to model and teach their children how to use technology responsibly and ethically. Just as Paul exhorts believers to *"Take captive every thought to make it obedient to Christ"* (2 Corinthians 10:5), we recognize the importance of guiding our children to discern between beneficial and harmful uses of digital technology. By setting boundaries around screen time, monitoring online content, and modeling healthy digital habits, we equip our children to navigate the digital landscape with wisdom, integrity, and discernment. As we incorporate principles of digital discipleship into our parenting practices, we instill in our children a sense of stewardship over their digital lives and a commitment to using technology as a tool for glorifying God and advancing His kingdom.

In conclusion, digital discipleship is integral to parenting in the digital age. By leveraging digital platforms and tools to engage our children in meaningful conversations about faith, connect them with a global community of believers, and teach them how to use technology responsibly, we empower them to grow as disciples of Christ and navigate the complexities of the digital world with wisdom and grace. As parents, we have a unique opportunity and responsibility to disciple our children in both the physical and digital realms, guiding them to walk in the footsteps of Jesus and shine His light in an increasingly digital and interconnected world.

> *"But be very careful! Never forget the things that you yourselves have seen. Remember these things for as long as you live. Tell your children and your grandchildren about all the things that God has done."*
>
> Deuteronomy 4:9 – Easy English Bible (EASY)

> *Just as Jesus used parables to teach His followers,*
> *"Through digital discipleship, we have the opportunity to*
> *engage with individuals across continents, sharing God's*
> *love and truth through the click of a button."*
>
> — Jabez Ministry

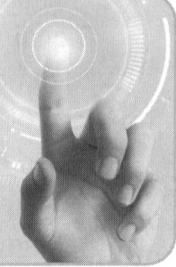

A. Raising Spiritually Aware Children

Have you ever wondered how our lives might have unfolded differently if we had been introduced to spirituality earlier? Many of us, as spiritual parents, often contemplate whether we can involve our children in our spiritual practices. Nancy Montgomery suggests that spirituality plays a crucial role in establishing a foundation to navigate challenging moments for our children. As our children mature, fostering strong bonds within family and community, along with a sense of purpose and achievement, can enhance their resilience in forging their life journey. There are simple ways to infuse spirituality into our children's lives. To assist parents in this endeavor, here are some guidelines for nurturing a spiritually grounded child.

1. **Start Early:** We should begin introducing spiritual concepts and practices to our children from a young age.

2. **Create Rituals:** Let's establish family rituals and traditions that emphasize spirituality, such as mealtime prayers or bedtime blessings.

3. **Practice Active Listening:** Let's listen attentively to our children's thoughts and questions about spirituality and provide thoughtful responses.

4. **Be Open-Minded:** We should maintain an open-minded attitude towards our children's spiritual journey, respecting their individual beliefs and experiences.

5. **Promote Self-Reflection:** We can encourage our children to reflect on their thoughts, feelings, and experiences, fostering self-awareness and introspection.

6. **Model Integrity:** Let's demonstrate honesty, integrity, and authenticity in our own spiritual practices and interactions.

7. **Provide Guidance:** Let's offer guidance and support as our children navigate spiritual questions and challenges, serving as trusted mentors and confidants.

8. **Engage in Nature:** We can spend time outdoors together, exploring the beauty of nature and fostering a sense of awe and wonder.

9. **Practice Mindfulness:** Let's teach our children mindfulness techniques such as deep breathing or meditation to help them cultivate presence and inner peace.

10. **Lead by Example:** We should live out our own spiritual values and beliefs in our daily lives, serving as positive role models for our children.

11. **Read Bible Texts:** Let's read stories and passages from bible texts together, discussing their meanings and relevance to our children's lives.

12. **Create Sacred Space:** Let's designate a special area in our home for prayer, meditation, or reflection, inviting our children to join us in spiritual practices.

13. **Encourage Creativity:** We can foster our children's creativity through art, music, storytelling, or other expressive outlets that allow them to explore spirituality in a creative way.

14. **Practice Forgiveness:** We should teach our children the importance of forgiveness and reconciliation, helping them learn to let go of resentments and cultivate inner peace.

15. **Encourage Volunteerism:** We can engage our children in volunteer activities or service projects that allow them to put their spiritual values into action and make a positive difference in the world.

16. **Emphasize Love:** We should teach our children that love is at the core of all spiritual traditions, encouraging them to cultivate love and compassion in their relationships and interactions.

17. **Offer Support:** We need to be there to support our children through spiritual struggles or doubts, offering guidance, encouragement, and reassurance along the way.

18. **Promote Connection:** Let's help our children develop a sense of connection to God rather than themselves for assurance of strength.

19. **Encourage Journaling:** We can encourage our children to keep a journal where they can record their thoughts, prayers, and spiritual experiences, providing a space for reflection and growth.

20. **Practice Simplicity:** We should emphasize the value of simplicity and moderation in our children's lives, teaching them to find joy and contentment in life's simple pleasures rather than material possessions.

By incorporating these tips into our parenting approach, we can help nurture a deep and meaningful spiritual life in our children, fostering their growth and development as spiritual beings.

> *"Listen, my child, when your father shows you what is right. And do not forget what your mother has taught you. Their teaching will bring you honour, like a beautiful crown or a valuable necklace."*
>
> Proverbs 1:8-9 – Easy English Bible (EASY)

> *"Blessed be childhood, which brings down something of heaven into the midst of our rough earthliness."*
>
> – Henri Frederic Amiel 1821 – 1881

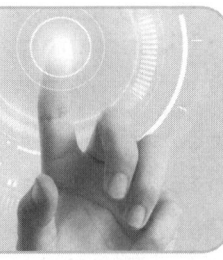

B. Family Devotions In A Digital Age

As Christian parents navigating the complexities of the digital age, we find ourselves both challenged and enriched in our journey of fostering family devotions. Our desire to cultivate a strong spiritual foundation within our households remains steadfast, yet we recognize the unique opportunities and obstacles presented by the pervasive presence of technology.

In embracing family devotions in a digital age, we acknowledge the importance of intentional engagement with our faith amidst the distractions of screens and devices. Our commitment to nurturing spiritual growth within our families compels us to set aside dedicated time for prayer, Bible study, and worship, free from the interruptions of digital media. By prioritizing these moments of connection with God and each other, we create sacred spaces where our faith can flourish.

However, we also recognize the allure of digital entertainment and the potential for technology to encroach upon our devotional practices. As parents, we strive to model discernment and moderation in our own use of technology, guiding our children in making wise choices about their online activities. By establishing boundaries and cultivating an atmosphere of reverence during family devotions, we seek to instill in our children a deep appreciation for the spiritual disciplines that sustain our faith.

Moreover, we embrace the wealth of resources available online as tools to enhance our family devotional life. From Bible apps and devotionals to Christian podcasts and streaming services, we leverage digital platforms to enrich our understanding of Scripture and engage with fellow believers. By actively seeking out edifying content and participating in virtual communities of faith, we strengthen our spiritual bonds as a family and draw closer to God together.

In essence, family devotions in a digital age require us to be intentional and proactive in nurturing our children's faith within the context of today's technological society. By integrating digital resources with traditional devotional practices and modeling discernment in our own digital habits, we strive to create a home environment where the love of God is central and where our family can flourish spiritually.

> *"Let the message about Christ completely fill your lives while you use all your wisdom to teach and instruct each other. With thankful hearts, sing psalms, hymns, and spiritual songs to God."*
>
> Colossians 3:16
> - Contemporary English Version (CEV)

"*Every Christian family should illustrate to the world the power and excellence of Christian influence. God designs that every family on earth shall be a symbol of the family in heaven, and parents should realize their accountability to keep their homes free from every taint of moral evil. Fathers and mothers should teach the infant, the child, and the youth about the love of Jesus. Let the first baby lispings be of Christ. The father, the priest of the family, if he is connected with God, will feel a divine charge to set himself apart for the grand and elevating work of saving the souls of his children.*"

– Review and Herald, October 9, 1900, par. 1

C. Online Faith Communities

As Christian parents, we recognize the importance of fostering a supportive community for ourselves and our children, even in the digital realm. In Hebrews 10:24-25, we are encouraged: "*And let us consider how we may spur one another on toward love and good deeds, not giving up meeting together, as some are in the habit of doing, but encouraging one another—and all the more as you see the Day approaching."* This verse emphasizes the significance of community in our faith journey, whether it be in physical gatherings or online interactions.

Engaging with online faith communities can offer invaluable support and resources for parenting in today's digital age. These communities provide a platform for us to connect with other Christian families, share experiences, and seek advice on raising our children in accordance with biblical principles. Through online forums, social media groups, or virtual Bible studies, we can find encouragement, solidarity, and practical wisdom from fellow believers who are navigating similar challenges and joys of parenting.

Online faith communities offer a diverse range of resources tailored specifically for parenting in the digital age. From curated content on family devotions and children's Bible studies to discussions on navigating technology use within the home, these platforms equip us with the tools and insights needed to raise our children in a spiritually nurturing environment amidst the pervasive influence of digital culture.

As we engage in online faith communities for parenting, we must exercise discernment and wisdom. Not all online platforms may align with our Christian values, and it's essential to carefully evaluate the content and interactions within these communities. We should prioritize communities that uphold biblical truth, promote genuine fellowship, and provide edifying resources for our families.

Additionally, while online interactions can supplement our faith journey, they should not replace the importance of physical fellowship and engagement within a local church community. We must strive to strike a balance between online and offline interactions, recognizing that both play complementary roles in nurturing our spiritual growth and that of our children.

In conclusion, online faith communities offer valuable support, resources, and fellowship for Christian parents navigating the challenges and opportunities of parenting in a digital age. By actively engaging with these communities while exercising discernment and maintaining a commitment to physical fellowship, we can cultivate a spiritually vibrant environment for our families to grow in faith.

Here are some suggestions for activities for online faith communities:

1. **Parenting Support Groups:** Encourage the establishment of online parenting support groups within faith communities, where Christian parents can connect, share experiences, seek advice, and pray for one another. These groups provide a platform for mutual encouragement, guidance, and solidarity in the journey of raising children in accordance with biblical principles.

2. **Digital Family Devotionals:** Create and share resources for digital family devotionals that cater to the specific needs and challenges of parenting in the digital age. These devotionals can include Bible readings, discussion questions, and activities designed to engage both parents and children in meaningful spiritual interactions within the home.

3. **Online Parenting Workshops and Seminars:** Organize online workshops and seminars focused on parenting from a Christian perspective, addressing topics such as instilling faith values, discipline, technology management, and fostering spiritual growth in children. These events provide opportunities for parents to learn from experts, exchange ideas, and gain practical insights for navigating the complexities of modern parenting.

4. **Virtual Parenting Accountability Groups:** Facilitate virtual parenting accountability groups where Christian parents commit to supporting and holding each other accountable in their parenting journey. These groups can provide a space for sharing successes, challenges, and prayer requests, fostering accountability and growth in parenting skills and spiritual leadership within the family.

5. **Digital Family Outreach Initiatives:** Engage in digital family outreach initiatives aimed at supporting and ministering to families beyond the immediate faith community. This can include online parenting blogs, social media campaigns, and webinars addressing common parenting issues from a Christian perspective, with the goal of reaching and impacting families outside traditional church circles.

By embracing these suggestions, Christian parents can leverage online faith communities as a resourceful and supportive environment for strengthening their parenting skills, nurturing their children's faith, and building a solid foundation of biblical values within their families.

"The Spirit of the Lord God is on me because the Lord has chosen me to bring good news to poor people. He has sent me to heal those with a sad heart. He has sent me to tell those who are being held and those in prison that they can go free."

Isaiah 61:1 - New Life Version (NLV)

"As believers, we are running the race together. We are connected by our faith in God and our love for the world that He sent Christ to save. So, if one gets weak, we carry them. We aren't called to stop moving forward. We aren't called to criticize each other. No, we are called to encourage each other, to reach down and carry each other, and to keep moving."

– Jesse Duplantis

CHAPTER VI

Navigating Challenges

As parents navigating the digital landscape, we are confronted with a myriad of challenges that test our resolve to raise our children in accordance with our Christian values. In today's technologically-driven society, the digital world presents both opportunities for growth and pitfalls that can hinder our children's spiritual development. How do we, as Christian parents, navigate these challenges while remaining steadfast in our faith?

First and foremost, we recognize that our role as parents is divinely ordained. In Ephesians 6:4, we are reminded to bring up our children in the training and instruction of the Lord. This biblical mandate extends to all aspects of our children's lives, including their digital interactions. Thus, we approach the challenges of parenting in the digital world with prayerful discernment, seeking guidance from God's Word and the wisdom of fellow believers.

One of the foremost challenges we face is the pervasive influence of technology on our children's lives. From social media platforms to online gaming, the digital realm offers a plethora of distractions that can divert our children's attention from their spiritual growth. As Christian parents, we must strike a balance between embracing technology for its educational and social benefits while safeguarding our children's spiritual well-being.

Central to our approach is the cultivation of discernment and wisdom in our children. Proverbs 2:6 tells us that the Lord gives wisdom, and from His mouth comes knowledge and understanding. Drawing from this biblical truth, we teach our children to critically evaluate digital content, discerning between that which aligns with our Christian values and that which does not. Through open dialogue and intentional guidance, we empower our children to make wise choices in their online interactions.

We address the issue of cyberbullying and online safety with both vigilance and compassion. In Matthew 5:44, Jesus instructs us to love our enemies and pray for those who persecute us. Applying this principle to the digital realm, we teach our children to respond to cyberbullying with grace and forgiveness, even as we take practical steps to ensure their safety online. By equipping them with strategies to protect themselves and seek help when needed, we instill in them a sense of resilience rooted in their faith.

In our journey of parenting spiritually in the digital world, we do not walk alone. We draw strength from our faith community, leaning on fellow believers for support and encouragement. Additionally, we avail ourselves of resources that offer practical guidance informed by Christian principles, such as "Tech Savvy Parenting" by Timothy Kimmel and "The Tech-Wise Family" by Andy Crouch.

In conclusion, navigating the challenges of parenting in the digital world requires a steadfast commitment to our Christian faith. By grounding our approach in prayer, biblical wisdom, and community support, we empower our children to thrive spiritually in an increasingly digital age.

> *"Be strong and have strength of heart. Do not be afraid or shake with fear because of them. For the Lord your God is the One Who goes with you. He will be faithful to you. He will not leave you alone."*
>
> Deuteronomy 31:6 - New Life Version (NLV)

> *"I may not be able to give my kids everything they want, but I give them what they need: love, time, and attention. You can't buy those things."*
>
> – Nishan Panwar

A. Cyberbullying And Online Safety

Cyberbullying refers to the use of digital communication tools, such as the internet, social media, or smartphones, to harass, intimidate, or harm others. It can take various forms, including sending hurtful messages, spreading rumors, sharing embarrassing photos or videos, and excluding individuals from online groups or communities. Cyberbullying can have serious consequences for victims, including emotional distress, depression, anxiety, and even suicidal thoughts or actions.

Online safety, on the other hand, encompasses measures and practices aimed at protecting individuals, particularly children and adolescents, from various online threats and risks. This includes safeguarding personal information, avoiding interactions with strangers, recognizing and reporting inappropriate content or behavior, and using privacy settings and security features effectively.

As parents navigating the digital world, it's crucial for us to address the issues of cyberbullying and online safety within a spiritual framework. Here's how we can approach these challenges:

1. **Raising Awareness and Educating Our Children**: Parents, educators, and caregivers are pivotal in fostering awareness about cyberbullying and imparting knowledge on online safety practices to young individuals. It is imperative to equip our children with the ability to identify cyberbullying behavior, comprehend its repercussions, and employ suitable responses. As parents, our responsibility lies in both raising awareness about cyberbullying and instilling in our children a deep understanding of online safety protocols. We must empower them to discern cyberbullying behavior, grasp its significance, and react appropriately, all while upholding our spiritual values of empathy and compassion.

2. **Fostering Open Communication:** Fostering open lines of communication with our children is essential for tackling

cyberbullying and ensuring online safety. Encourage our children to confide in trusted adults should they face cyberbullying or come across questionable content online. Cultivating a secure environment for dialogue enables our children to feel supported and empowered to seek assistance when necessary. We aim to establish transparent communication channels with our children, urging them to share any experiences of cyberbullying or discomfort online. Through nurturing a safe and trusting space for conversation, we can assist our children in navigating the intricate landscape of the digital realm while upholding our spiritual values.

3. **Setting Boundaries and Monitoring:** We recognize the importance of setting boundaries regarding our children's online activities and screen time, emphasizing the need for balance and moderation. Implementing parental controls and monitoring software allows us to track our children's online behavior and intervene if we detect any risks or threats to their well-being. Parents can set boundaries regarding their children's online activities and screen time, balancing their digital interactions with real-world experiences. This approach ensures that our children develop healthy habits and stay safe in their online endeavors.

4. **Promoting Positive Online Behavior:** Our aim is to instill in our children the values of responsible and respectful online behavior, rooted in our spiritual beliefs of love and kindness towards others. We emphasize the importance of treating others with dignity and respect, both online and offline, and encourage our children to be mindful of their digital footprint. Teach our children about responsible and respectful online behavior, emphasizing the golden rule of treating others as they would like to be treated. Encourage empathy, kindness, and digital citizenship, both in interactions with peers and when engaging with online content. This approach ensures that our children navigate the digital world with integrity and compassion.

5. **Seeking Support and Intervention:** If our children experience cyberbullying, it's crucial to take immediate action to address the situation. This may involve reporting the abuse to the relevant platform or service provider, documenting evidence of the cyberbullying, and seeking support from school authorities, counselors, or law enforcement if necessary. We instill in our children the importance of standing up against injustice while embodying the principles of forgiveness and reconciliation in our actions.

6. **Accessing Resources and Support Networks:** As spiritually guided parents in the digital era, we understand the importance of accessing resources and support networks to ensure our children's well-being online. We actively seek guidance and assistance, utilizing online guides, educational materials, and community forums to stay informed about digital safety and combat cyberbullying. Building a strong support network with fellow parents, educators, and mental health professionals who share our values is a priority. Together, we work towards creating a safe and nurturing digital environment where our children can flourish, all while upholding our spiritual principles of empathy, compassion, and integrity.

Here are some references and resources for further information on cyberbullying and online safety:

https://www.stopbullying.gov/resources/get-help-now

https://www.pacer.org/bullying/info/cyberbullying/

https://cyberbullying.org/

https://www.icactaskforce.org/internetsafety

> *"Brothers and sisters, if a person is caught doing something wrong, you who are spiritual should restore someone like this with a spirit of gentleness. Watch out for yourselves so you won't be tempted too."*

Galatians 6:1- Common English Bible (CEB)

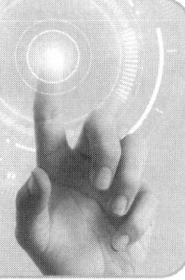

> *"I am a huge advocate for anti-bullying in our youth. What I have seen with the rise of social media is that children are not facing bullying on a playground; they are facing it on their cell phones."*
>
> – Whitney Wolfe Herd

B. Screen Time Management

In adopting a Christian psychology approach to raising our children, we recognize the significance of nurturing their spiritual, emotional, and psychological well-being. As parents, we understand that screen time management plays a crucial role in shaping our children's development, and we approach this aspect of parenting with intentionality and prayerful discernment.

We acknowledge the importance of balance in our children's screen time usage. Just as Ecclesiastes 3:1 reminds us that there is a time for everything, including technology, we strive to instill in our children a sense of moderation and self-control when it comes to engaging with screens. This means setting clear boundaries and limits on their screen time, ensuring that it does not overshadow other important activities such as family time, outdoor play, and spiritual practices.

We recognize that excessive screen time can have detrimental effects on our children's mental and emotional well-being. Proverbs 4:23 admonishes us to guard our hearts, for everything we do flows from it. Applying this wisdom to screen time management, we prioritize protecting our children's minds from harmful content and negative influences online. This may involve monitoring their screen usage, implementing parental controls, and guiding them toward wholesome and edifying digital content that aligns with our Christian values.

We view screen time management as an opportunity to foster meaningful connections within our family. Instead of allowing screens to divide us, we use technology as a tool for bonding and quality time together. Whether it's watching a family-friendly movie, playing educational games, or participating in virtual Bible studies, we seek to leverage screen time in ways that strengthen our family relationships and deepen our children's spiritual formation.

In addition, we approach screen time management with a spirit of discernment, recognizing that not all screen activities are created equal. Just as Philippians 4:8 instructs us to dwell on whatever is true, noble, right, pure, lovely, and admirable, we encourage our children to engage in screen activities that uplift and inspire them. This may involve introducing them to faith-based apps, educational programs, or wholesome entertainment that reinforce biblical values and promote spiritual growth.

Ultimately, our approach to screen time management is guided by our faith in God and our desire to raise our children in a way that honors Him. By integrating Christian principles into our parenting practices, we equip our children with the tools they need to navigate the digital world with wisdom, discernment, and a strong foundation in their faith.

Here are some suggestions for managing screen time effectively:

1. **Set Clear Boundaries:** Establish clear rules and guidelines regarding when and for how long screens can be used each day.

Communicate these boundaries to our children and enforce them consistently.

2. **Lead by Example:** Model healthy screen time habits for our children by limiting our own screen use and engaging in alternative activities such as reading, outdoor play, or family interactions.

3. **Encourage Alternative Activities:** Provide our children with alternative activities to screen time, such as playing board games, doing arts and crafts, or engaging in physical exercise. Encourage them to explore their interests and hobbies offline.

4. **Use Screen Time as a Reward:** Make screen time contingent on completing chores, homework, or other responsibilities. This helps reinforce the idea that screen time is a privilege to be earned rather than a right.

5. **Encourage Outdoor Play:** Encourage your children to spend time outdoors engaging in physical activity and exploring nature. Limiting screen time can help promote physical health and overall well-being.

By implementing these suggestions, you can help your family develop healthy screen time habits and strike a balance between technology use and other meaningful activities.

"For everything, there is an appointed time. There is an appropriate time for every activity under heaven."

Ecclesiastes 3:1
- Evangelical Heritage Version (EHV)

> *"Speak with your children as if they are the wisest, kindest, most beautiful humans on earth, for what they believe is what they will become."*
>
> – Brooke Hampton

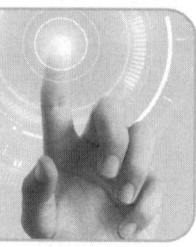

C. Digital Addiction

Digital addiction, also known as internet addiction or technology addiction, refers to the compulsive and excessive use of digital devices and online activities, leading to negative consequences in various areas of life. Similar to other forms of addiction, such as substance abuse, gambling, or gaming addiction, digital addiction involves a loss of control over one's behavior despite awareness of its detrimental effects.

The consequences of digital addiction can be far-reaching and impact various aspects of an individual's life, including:

- Impaired academic or work performance due to distraction and procrastination.
- Disruption of sleep patterns and disturbances in circadian rhythms.
- Decline in physical health due to sedentary behavior and neglect of self-care.
- Strained interpersonal relationships, isolation, and loneliness.
- Mental health issues such as anxiety, depression, and low self-esteem.
- Financial problems related to excessive spending on digital subscriptions, in-app purchases, or online gambling.

As parents committed to guiding our children in a spiritually healthy manner, we recognize the significance of incorporating spiritual practices into our approach to addressing digital addiction. Here's how we can integrate these practices into our parenting:

1. **Prayer and Meditation:** Together as a family, we begin and end each day with prayer and meditation, seeking God's guidance and strength to overcome digital addiction. We model the importance of relying on God's wisdom and power in all aspects of our lives, including our digital habits.

2. **Scripture Reading**: We encourage our children to spend time reading and reflecting on Scripture daily, allowing God's Word to renew their minds and provide wisdom in managing digital habits. Through regular engagement with Scripture, we equip them with spiritual insights to navigate the challenges of the digital world.

3. **Worship and Praise**: We engage in worship and praise together through music, singing, and creative expression, lifting our hearts and souls to God beyond the confines of digital screens. Worship becomes a central part of our family life, strengthening our bond with each other and with God.

4. **Nature Connection**: We prioritize spending time in nature as a family, marveling at God's creation and finding solace and peace away from digital devices. Nature serves as a reminder of God's majesty and power, grounding us in His presence and restoring our souls.

5. **Setting Spiritual Goals:** Together, we set spiritual goals aligned with God's purposes for our lives, focusing on growth, service, and discipleship rather than digital distractions. By setting our minds on things above, we cultivate a Kingdom-focused perspective in our family life.

6. **Digital Fasting:** We periodically fast from specific digital platforms, apps, or forms of entertainment that contribute to digital addiction, redirecting our focus towards spiritual growth. Through digital fasting, we break free from unhealthy patterns and renew our commitment to God.

7. **Trusting in God's Provision:** Ultimately, we trust in God's provision and grace as we seek to overcome digital addiction,

knowing that He is faithful to guide us towards spiritual freedom and abundant life in Him. By placing our trust in God, we find strength and hope for the journey ahead.

By implementing these spiritual practices within our family, we create a nurturing and supportive environment where we can grow together in faith and overcome digital addiction. With God's help and the support of one another, we can break free from the grip of digital distractions and live lives that honor and glorify Him.

> *"So let God work His will in you. Yell a loud no to the Devil and watch him make himself scarce. Say a quiet yes to God, and He'll be there in no time. Quit dabbling in sin. Purify your inner life. Quit playing the field. Hit bottom, and cry your eyes out. The fun and games are over. Get serious, really serious. Get down on your knees before the Master; it's the only way you'll get on your feet."*

James 4:7-10 - The Message (MSG)

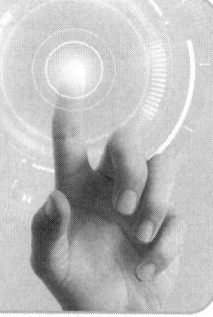

> *"The addiction to using digital devices and social media on the internet will surely have negative effects on health. And will distance the relationship between parents and their children, as well as their relationship with God."*
>
> – Ed Japlit

CHAPTER VII
Creating A Digital Covenant

As parents navigating the intricacies of raising children in a digital age, we are acutely aware of the profound impact that technology can have on our families' lives. In our journey to instill values and principles that align with our Christian faith, we recognize the necessity of creating a digital covenant—a set of guidelines and commitments that govern our family's use of technology. In doing so, we aim to foster a healthy, balanced, and God-honoring digital environment for ourselves and our children.

Central to our approach to creating a digital covenant is the recognition of technology's potential to shape our thoughts, behaviors, and relationships. Just as the apostle Paul admonishes in Romans 12:2 not to conform to the patterns of this world but to be transformed by the renewing of our minds, we understand the importance of intentional discernment and stewardship in our digital interactions. Thus, we embark on this journey with prayerful consideration and a desire to align our digital habits with our Christian values.

Our digital covenant begins with a family discussion—a collaborative effort involving every member, regardless of age. We recognize the importance of engaging our children in these conversations and valuing their input, concerns, and perspectives. Together, we identify core values such as integrity, respect, responsibility, and stewardship, which serve as the foundation upon which our digital covenant is built. By involving our children in this process, we empower them to take ownership of their digital habits and understand the significance of living out their faith in all areas of life.

Drawing inspiration from Scripture, we establish clear boundaries and guidelines for digital usage within our family. Just as Proverbs 4:25-27 urges us to *"Let your eyes look directly forward, and your gaze is straight before you,"* we set forth rules regarding screen time limits, appropriate content, online behavior, and device usage in certain locations or times of the day. These boundaries are not meant to restrict or control but rather to provide a framework for healthy and responsible digital engagement rooted in our Christian values.

As parents, we understand the importance of leading by example. We recognize that our actions speak louder than words, and thus, we strive to model healthy digital habits for our children to emulate. Whether it be prioritizing face-to-face interactions over digital communication, setting aside designated times for device-free activities, or practicing mindful consumption of digital content, we demonstrate the importance of balance, self-discipline, and discernment in our own use of technology.

Furthermore, we cultivate a culture of accountability within our family—a mutual commitment to uphold the standards outlined in our digital covenant. We encourage open communication, honest dialogue, and support for one another as we navigate the challenges of living in a digital world. Just as Ecclesiastes 4:9-10 reminds us that *"Two are better than one... for if they fall, one will lift up his fellow,"* we recognize the value of walking together in faith and mutual support.

Periodically, we engage in reflection and evaluation of our digital covenant as a family. We recognize that circumstances may change, challenges may arise, and adjustments may be necessary. Thus, we approach this process with humility, flexibility, and a willingness to learn and grow together. Through prayer, discussion, and discernment, we seek God's guidance in refining and strengthening our digital covenant to better reflect His will for our family.

In conclusion, creating a digital covenant within our family is not merely about setting rules and restrictions—it is about cultivating a holistic approach to digital stewardship rooted in our Christian faith. By establishing clear boundaries, modeling healthy habits, fostering accountability, and seeking God's guidance, we strive to create a nurturing and God-honoring digital environment for our family to flourish. In doing so, we affirm our commitment to living out our faith in every aspect of our lives, including our interactions with technology.

> *"Therefore, as God's chosen people, holy and dearly loved, clothe yourselves with compassion, kindness, humility, gentleness and patience. Bear with each other and forgive one another if any of you has a grievance against someone. Forgive as the Lord forgave you. And over all these virtues put on love, which binds them all together in perfect unity."*
>
> Colossians 3:12-14
> - New International Version (NIV)

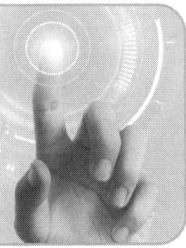

> *"The digital world isn't inherently negative if we use it wisely. However, if we allow it to dominate our lives, it can worsen our circumstances."*
>
> – Jabez Ministry

A. Setting Family Guideline

In navigating parenting in the digital world, setting family guidelines is paramount for ensuring a healthy balance between online engagement and real-life interactions. As parents, we recognize the importance of establishing clear boundaries and expectations regarding screen time, social media use, and online safety. By collectively establishing these guidelines as a family, we foster open communication and mutual understanding of the values we uphold in our digital interactions.

Together, we discuss the appropriate amount of time our children spend on devices and agree on designated tech-free zones and times within our home. We emphasize the importance of maintaining offline hobbies and spending quality time together as a family without distractions from screens. Additionally, we prioritize teaching our children about online safety, including the importance of privacy settings, discerning trustworthy sources, and being cautious of sharing personal information.

Through ongoing dialogue and reinforcement of these guidelines, we aim to empower our children to make responsible decisions in their digital lives while nurturing strong connections within our family unit. In today's fast-paced and digitally-driven world, we, as Christian parents, are confronted with the challenging responsibility of shepherding our children through the digital age.

Given the ever-expanding reach of technology and the internet, it's imperative for us to arm ourselves with strategies that guarantee our children's safe and responsible engagement with digital resources.

Here are some suggestions for establishing family guidelines:

1. **Christ-Like Behavior:** We strive to exemplify Christ-like behavior in our interactions with our children and in the way we guide them through life. We understand that Jesus embodied qualities such as love, kindness, compassion, forgiveness, and humility, which serve as guiding principles for our family. Our goal as parents is to raise children who embody the values and principles of Jesus Christ so that they may become compassionate, responsible, and faithful individuals who positively impact the world around them.

2. **Regular Family Prayer And Bible Study:** We place great importance on incorporating regular family prayer and Bible study into our routine. We believe that nurturing our children's spiritual development is essential for their overall well-being and growth. Regular family prayer and Bible study are integral components

of our parenting approach, helping us to cultivate a strong, faith-centered foundation for our children and nurture their spiritual growth in a loving and supportive environment.

3. **Set Clear Boundaries:** As parents, we need to define clear guidelines concerning screen time, content consumption, and device usage. Consistency is key; let's establish routines that strike a balance between technology usage and other activities such as physical play, reading, and social interactions. By setting boundaries, we, as parents, can help our children comprehend the significance of moderation and time management within the digital world.

4. **Educate About Online Safety:** As parents, let's educate our children on online safety, privacy, and responsible behavior. We should engage in conversations about the potential risks linked with sharing personal information and interacting with strangers online. Let's promote the adoption of strong, unique passwords and emphasize the significance of verifying the authenticity of websites and apps before disclosing any information.

5. **Open Communication and Honesty:** We encourage our children to communicate openly with us, knowing that we will listen to them without judgment and provide support when needed. We strive to cultivate trust through honest and transparent interactions, modeling integrity and authenticity in our own behavior. By engaging in open dialogue, we address misunderstandings, resolve conflicts, and strengthen our family bonds.

> *"Children, it is your Christian duty to obey your parents always, for that is what pleases God."*
>
> Colossians 3:20 - Good News Translation (GNT)

B. Technology And Responsibility

As Christian parents, we understand our duty as stewards of the resources and gifts bestowed upon us by God, which include the advancements in technology. In the book of Genesis 1:28, we are reminded of our responsibility to exercise dominion over the earth and all its inhabitants: *"God blessed them and said to them, 'Be fruitful and increase in number; fill the earth and subdue it. Rule over the fish in the sea and the birds in the sky and over every living creature that moves on the ground.'"*

As parents navigating the digital world, we acknowledge the significance of guiding our children in the prudent and ethical use of technology. In Proverbs 22:6, we are instructed, *"Train up a child in the way he should go; even when he is old, he will not depart from it."* This verse underscores our duty as parents to instill values and principles that will guide our children's choices, including their use of technology.

In today's digital age, technology plays a significant role in our children's lives, offering both opportunities and challenges. As responsible stewards of God's gift of parenthood, we are called to equip our children with the knowledge and discernment necessary to navigate the digital landscape with wisdom and integrity.

Ephesians 6:4 reminds us, *"Fathers, do not provoke your children to anger, but bring them up in the discipline and instruction of the Lord."* This verse emphasizes the importance of nurturing our children in a manner that reflects God's love and guidance. In the context of technology, this includes setting boundaries, fostering open communication, and providing guidance on how to use digital tools responsibly.

As parents, we are also called to lead by example in our own use of technology. Philippians 4:9 encourages us, *"Whatever you have learned or received or heard from me, or seen in me—put it into practice. And the God of peace will be with you."* Our children learn not only from our words but also from our actions. By modeling healthy digital habits and demonstrating self-control in our use of technology, we can provide a positive example for our children to follow.

Additionally, we must remain vigilant in monitoring our children's online activities and ensuring their safety in digital spaces. Proverbs 4:23 advises, *"Above all else, guard your heart, for everything you do flows from it."* This admonition reminds us of the importance of safeguarding our children's hearts and minds, even in the digital realm. By staying informed, setting age-appropriate restrictions, and engaging in ongoing conversations about online safety, we can fulfill our responsibility to protect and nurture our children in the digital world.

Ultimately, as Christian parents, our goal is to raise children who honor God in all aspects of their lives, including their use of technology. By grounding our parenting in biblical principles of love, wisdom, and responsibility, we can help our children develop a healthy relationship with technology that glorifies God and contributes to their spiritual growth and well-being.

Here are seven suggestions for parenting spiritually in the digital age, focusing on technology and responsibility:

1. **Pray Together:** Foster a culture of prayer in your family, praying together for God's guidance, protection, and wisdom in navigating the digital world responsibly.

2. **Explore Biblical Content:** Explore digital platforms that offer age-appropriate Bible stories, devotions, and educational materials to nurture your children's faith.

3. **Promote Digital Detox:** Encourage regular breaks from screens and engage in offline activities as a family, such as outdoor play, reading, or hobbies.

4. **Integrate Faith into Technology Use:** Incorporate faith-based apps, websites, and online resources into your family's digital routine to reinforce spiritual growth and learning.

5. **Lead by Example**: Let your children see you prioritize prayer, scripture reading, and spiritual growth over digital distractions, demonstrating the importance of faith in your life.

6. **Establish Technology Guidelines:** Set clear guidelines for the use of digital devices, including screen time limits, appropriate content, and online behavior.

7. **Prioritize Family Time**: Dedicate quality time for family activities without screens, such as meals, outings, and devotional times, to strengthen family bonds and spiritual connections.

> *"If you know what is right to do but you do not do it, you sin."*

James 4:17 - New Life Version (NLV)

"Our duty as parents is to guide our children through the digital world with wisdom, discernment, and a firm commitment to God's teachings. By instilling values of responsibility and faith, we empower them to use technology as a tool for spreading goodness and light in a world often overshadowed by darkness."

– Ed Japlit

C. Balancing Online And Offline Life

As Christian parents navigating the challenges of parenting in the digital world, we recognize the importance of striking a balance between online and offline life. In Ecclesiastes 3:1 (NIV), we're reminded, *"There is a time for everything and a season for every activity under the heavens."* This verse underscores the significance of balance and moderation in all aspects of life, including our use of technology.

In our family, we strive to uphold this principle by establishing clear boundaries and routines that promote a healthy balance between online and offline activities. Just as Ecclesiastes 3:1 suggests, there is a time for engaging with digital devices for educational, recreational, or social purposes, but there is also a time for unplugging and reconnecting with one another and with God.

We find guidance in Psalm 90:12 (NIV), which says, *"Teach us to number our days, that we may gain a heart of wisdom."* This verse reminds us of the importance of being intentional with our time and prioritizing activities that nourish our souls and strengthen our family bonds. By setting aside dedicated times for offline activities such as family meals, outdoor adventures, or devotional practices, we create opportunities for meaningful connections and spiritual growth.

Proverbs 4:25-27 (NIV) also advises, *"Let your eyes look straight ahead; fix your gaze directly before you. Give careful thought to the paths for your feet and be steadfast in all your ways. Do not turn to the right or the left; keep your foot from evil."* This passage encourages us to maintain focus and discernment in our choices, including our use of technology. By being mindful of the impact of excessive screen time on our family dynamics and spiritual well-being, we can make intentional decisions to prioritize offline experiences that nurture our relationships and deepen our faith.

Ultimately, our goal as Christian parents is to raise children who are connected to the Word of God, deeply grounded in our relationship with our Lord God and Savior Jesus Christ, and guided by the Holy Spirit. We aim to equip them to navigate the complexities of the digital world with wisdom, discernment, and a strong foundation in their faith. By balancing online and offline life according to biblical principles, we endeavor to cultivate a family culture that honors God in all that we do.

Here are ten suggestions on parenting spiritually in the digital world, accompanied by corresponding Bible verses about balancing online and offline life:

1. **Seek God's Guidance:** Pray for wisdom and discernment in parenting decisions, including those related to technology (James 1:5).

2. **Promote Face-to-Face Interaction:** Encourage in-person conversations and relationships to deepen connections (Proverbs 27:17).

3. **Teach Time Management:** Help children manage their time effectively, balancing screen time with other activities (Ephesians 5:15-17).

4. **Engage in Offline Worship:** Participate in offline worship activities such as church services and prayer meetings (Hebrews 10:24-25).

5. **Encourage Rest:** Emphasize the importance of rest and rejuvenation, both physically and spiritually (Matthew 11:28-30).

6. **Encourage Reading:** Promote reading physical books and literature to enhance cognitive development (Proverbs 4:7).

7. **Encourage Offline Hobbies:** Support children in developing offline hobbies and interests outside of screens (Ecclesiastes 3:22).

8. **Teach Self-Control:** Help children develop self-control in their technology use (Galatians 5:22-23).

9. **Emphasize Real-Life Connections:** Highlight the value of real-life relationships over virtual connections (John 13:34-35).

10.Discuss Digital Temptations: Have open conversations about the temptations and pitfalls of the digital world (1 Corinthians 10:13).

> *"Blessed (happy, fortunate, prosperous, and enviable) is the man who walks and lives not in the counsel of the ungodly [following their advice, their plans and purposes], nor stands [submissive and inactive] in the path where sinners walk, nor sits down [to relax and rest] where the scornful [and the mockers] gather. But his delight and desire are in the law of the Lord, and on His law (the precepts, the instructions, the teachings of God) he habitually meditates (ponders and studies) by day and by night."*
>
> Psalm 1:1-2
> - Amplified Bible, Classic Edition (AMPC)

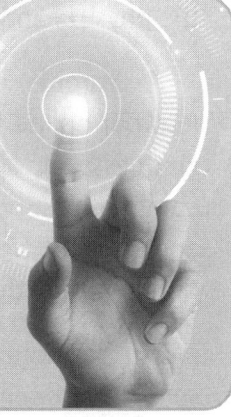

"*Parenting spiritually entails teaching our children to navigate the vast sea of the internet while keeping their hearts connected, grounded, and guided by the solid foundation of God's Word. It's about finding a delicate balance between the digital and the divine, ensuring that every step resonates with the melody of God's love.*"

– Jeb J. Bersabal

CHAPTER VIII

Faith In Action

Faith in Action is a fundamental concept in Christianity that emphasizes the dynamic relationship between belief and behavior. It asserts that genuine faith is not merely a passive acceptance of doctrine but a living, active force that manifests itself through deeds of love, compassion, and obedience to God's will. This concept is deeply rooted in various passages throughout the Bible, which underscore the inseparable connection between faith and action.

Parenting spiritually in the digital age presents unique challenges and opportunities as we strive to instill in our children the values of our faith while navigating the vast landscape of technology. In this digital realm, the concept of Faith in Action remains as relevant as ever, emphasizing the dynamic relationship between belief and behavior.

Drawing inspiration from James 2:14-17, we guide our children to understand that genuine faith extends beyond mere words or beliefs—it is reflected in our actions. Through meaningful conversations and practical examples, we teach them that faith in action involves actively demonstrating love, compassion, and obedience to God's will in both the physical and digital realms.

As parents, we model Faith in Action by integrating our beliefs into our online interactions and digital habits. Whether it's spreading kindness and positivity on social media, participating in virtual community service projects, or using technology to advocate for justice and equality, we demonstrate to our children that faith transcends the boundaries of the digital world and permeates every aspect of our lives.

Furthermore, we actively engage our children in acts of digital service and compassion, encouraging them to use technology as a tool for spreading love and making a positive impact. Whether it's supporting online fundraisers for charitable causes, participating in virtual volunteer opportunities, or using their online platforms to raise awareness about important issues, we empower our children to be agents of change in the digital sphere.

In our efforts to parent spiritually in the digital age, we continually reinforce the principle of Faith in Action through intentional conversations and reflection. We encourage our children to critically evaluate their online behaviors and digital interactions, guiding them to discern how their faith informs their online presence and digital engagement.

By nurturing a deep understanding of the inseparable connection between faith and action, both online and offline, we equip our children to navigate the complexities of the digital world with integrity, compassion, and a steadfast commitment to living out their faith in meaningful ways. As they grow and flourish in their spiritual journey, they become empowered to harness the power of technology for good, making a positive impact in their communities and the world at large.

> *"So you see, it isn't enough just to have faith. You must also do good to prove that you have it. Faith that doesn't show itself by good works is no faith at all—it is dead and useless."*
>
> James 2:17- Living Bible (TLB)

> *"With God, you are stronger than your struggles and more fierce than your fears. God provides comfort and strength to those who trust in Him. Be encouraged, keep standing, and know that everything's going to be alright. Never give up. Things may be hard, but if you quit trying, they'll never get better. Stop worrying and start trusting God. It will be worth it."*
>
> – Germany Kent

A. Practicing Compassion And Kindness Online

As parents navigating the digital world, we recognize the importance of instilling values of compassion and kindness in our children's online interactions. In today's interconnected society, our digital footprint often extends beyond physical boundaries, shaping the way we engage with others and contribute to online communities. Drawing inspiration from biblical principles, we strive to guide our children in practicing compassion and kindness in the digital sphere.

One key aspect of parenting spiritually in the digital world is teaching our children to treat others with empathy and respect, even in virtual spaces. Just as Jesus emphasized the importance of loving our neighbors as ourselves (Matthew 22:39), we encourage our children to extend kindness and compassion to everyone they encounter online. Whether it's responding to comments with grace and understanding or refraining from participating in cyberbullying, we emphasize the importance of treating others with dignity and empathy, regardless of differences.

Furthermore, we seek to model compassionate behavior in our own online interactions, recognizing that our actions serve as powerful examples for our children. Just as Ephesians 4:32 encourages us to be kind and compassionate to one another, forgiving each other as God forgave us, we strive to embody these values in our digital communication. By demonstrating patience, empathy, and understanding in our online interactions, we show our children that compassion is not just a virtue to be practiced in the physical world but an essential component of our digital citizenship as well.

In addition to modeling compassionate behavior, we actively encourage our children to engage in acts of kindness and service online. Whether it's reaching out to a friend in need through a supportive message or participating in online campaigns for social justice causes, we empower our children to use their digital platforms as tools for making a positive difference in the world. Just as Galatians 6:10 urges us to do good to all people, especially to those who belong to the family of believers, we teach our children that their online presence can be a source of light and hope in a world often marked by negativity and division.

Moreover, we emphasize the importance of digital discernment, teaching our children to critically evaluate the impact of their online actions and words. Proverbs 16:24 reminds us that gracious words are like a honeycomb, sweet to the soul and healing to the bones. By encouraging our children to pause and reflect before posting or sharing content online, we help them cultivate a digital presence characterized by kindness, empathy, and positivity.

In conclusion, parenting spiritually in the digital world involves guiding our children to practice compassion and kindness in their online interactions. Through modeling compassionate behavior, encouraging acts of kindness and service, and promoting digital discernment, we equip our children to navigate the complexities of the digital realm with integrity and grace. As we strive to raise children who embody the values of compassion and kindness both online and offline, we fulfill our calling to be agents of love and transformation in the digital age.

> *"Be kind and compassionate to one another, forgiving each other, just as in Christ God forgave you."*
>
> Ephesians 4:32 - New International Version (NIV)

> *"While the Christian will be ever kind, compassionate, and forgiving, he can feel no harmony with sin… The spirit of Christ will lead us to hate sin while we are willing to make any sacrifice to save the sinner."*
>
> – Testimonies for the Church vol. 5 p. 171 (1882)

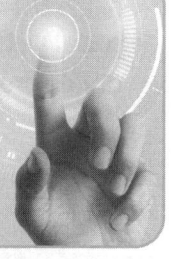

B. Acts Of Service In A Digital World

As parents, we understand the importance of instilling values of service and compassion in our children's online interactions. In today's interconnected society, opportunities for acts of service extend beyond physical boundaries, offering unique avenues for making a positive impact in the digital sphere. Drawing inspiration from biblical principles and the teachings of our Lord Jesus Christ, we endeavor to guide our children in engaging in acts of service and kindness online.

One crucial element of spiritual parenting in the digital era is instilling in our children the value of using their online presence to serve others. Just as Jesus highlighted the significance of serving others in Mark 10:45, we encourage our children to explore ways to extend kindness and assistance through digital platforms. This might entail activities like engaging in virtual mentorship programs, offering free educational resources, or collaborating on creative projects that inspire positivity and unity in online communities. By empowering our children to harness technology as a means of service, we equip them to embody the principles of compassion and generosity in the digital world, contributing to a culture of empathy and support online.

Furthermore, we model acts of service in our own online interactions, demonstrating to our children the importance of using our digital presence to uplift and support others. Just as Philippians 2:4 encourages us to look not only to our own interests but also to the interests of others, we strive to prioritize acts of service and kindness in our digital engagements. Whether it's offering words of encouragement to someone in need, sharing valuable resources or information, or actively participating in online communities dedicated to service and social justice, we exemplify the values of compassion and service in our online presence.

In addition to modeling acts of service, we actively engage our children in digital service projects and initiatives, offering them opportunities to contribute to causes they care deeply about. For instance, they may collaborate on creating informative podcasts to educate others about mental health, organize virtual cleanup events to promote environmental awareness or participate in online petitions advocating for animal rights. Through these endeavors, we empower our children to harness their talents and resources to bring about positive change in the digital sphere, fostering a sense of responsibility and activism in the online community.

Moreover, we emphasize the importance of using digital platforms responsibly and ethically in acts of service. Just as Ephesians 4:29 urges us to speak only what is helpful for building others up according to their needs, we teach our children to use their online voices to spread positivity, kindness, and encouragement. By practicing digital discernment and critical thinking, we guide them to engage in acts of service that are aligned with their values and beliefs while also respecting the dignity and privacy of others.

In conclusion, parenting spiritually in the digital world involves guiding our children to engage in acts of service and kindness in the online realm. Through modeling acts of service, involving our children in digital service projects, and emphasizing responsible digital citizenship, we equip them to leverage technology as a tool for making a positive difference in the world. As we cultivate a culture of service and compassion in our digital interactions, we fulfill our calling to be agents of love and transformation in the digital age.

"Feed the hungry! Help those in trouble! Then your light will shine out from the darkness, and the darkness around you shall be as bright as day."

Isaiah 58:10 - Living Bible (TLB)

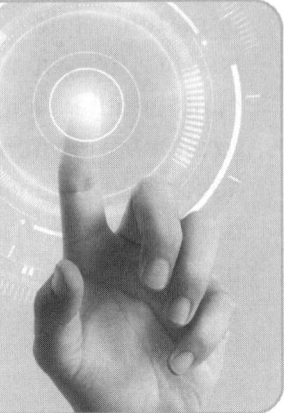

> *"Let the youth remember that here they are to build characters for eternity and that God requires them to do their best. Let those older in experience watch over the younger ones, and when they see them tempted, take them aside and pray with them and for them."*
>
> – Messages to Young People, p.18.1

C. Parenting As A Spiritual Journey

As we navigate the challenges of parenting in the digital world, we recognize that it is not just about managing screen time or monitoring online activities. Parenting in the digital age is also a spiritual journey—one that requires us to guide our children in developing a strong moral compass, nurturing their spiritual growth, and helping them navigate the complexities of the digital landscape in a way that aligns with our faith values.

Just as the Bible emphasizes the importance of raising children in the ways of the Lord (Proverbs 22:6), we view parenting as a sacred responsibility entrusted to us by God. We understand that our role extends beyond providing material needs to shaping our children's hearts and souls, teaching them to love God and others in both the physical and digital realms.

As we embark on this spiritual journey of parenting in the digital age, we draw inspiration from biblical principles and teachings. For example, Deuteronomy 6:6-7 instructs us to impress God's commandments on our children's hearts and to talk about them when we sit at home, when we walk along the road, when we lie down, and when we get up. In the context of the digital world, this means actively engaging our children in conversations about faith, love, hope, forgiveness, ethics, and responsible online behavior, integrating spiritual teachings into their daily lives and digital experiences.

Furthermore, parenting as a spiritual journey in the digital age entails exemplifying faith and integrity in our own online interactions. Just as 1 Timothy 4:12 encourages believers to be models in speech, conduct, love, faith, and purity, we endeavor to showcase values of honesty, kindness, and compassion in our digital presence. Whether it involves refraining from sharing divisive content on social media, exercising digital discernment in our online engagements, or using our platforms to disseminate messages of hope and encouragement, we strive to embody the principles of our faith and the love of our Lord God, Jesus Christ, in the digital realm.

Additionally, parenting as a spiritual journey in the digital age requires us to foster open communication and trust with our children. We create a safe space for them to share their questions, concerns, and experiences online, guiding them with wisdom and love. Just as Ephesians 6:4 admonishes parents not to exasperate their children but to bring them up in the training and instruction of the Lord God Jesus Christ, we strive to provide guidance and support rooted in faith and understanding of God's word.

In conclusion, parenting in the digital world is a spiritual journey that encompasses guiding our children in faith, integrity, and responsible digital citizenship. By drawing on biblical principles, modeling faith in our own online interactions, and fostering open communication and trust, we equip our children to navigate the digital landscape with wisdom, discernment, and a strong foundation of faith. As we walk alongside them on this journey, we seek to instill in them a deep love for God and a commitment to living out their faith in every aspect of their lives, both online and offline.

> *"Punishment and discipline can make children wise, but children who are never corrected will bring shame to their mothers."*

Proverbs 29:15 - Easy-to-Read Version (ERV)

> *"Jesus Christ is a "tried stone." Those who trust in Him, He never disappoints."*
>
> – Ellen G. White, The Desire of Ages

CHAPTER IX

Case Studies

A. Real-Life Examples Of Spiritually Grounded Parenting In The Digital Age

Our family of four lived harmoniously in different places here and abroad. My wife Ellen and I, as parents devoted to our two sons, Hans and Ace, embarked on a journey of faith from the moment our sons entered the world. Together, we made it our mission to introduce them to the word of God. We began each day with morning worship, delving into Bible stories, the life and teachings of our Lord God and Savior Jesus Christ, and sharing prayers as a family. In the evenings, we reconvened for another session of worship, reflecting on our day and expressing gratitude for the blessings bestowed upon us.

As Hans and Ace matured, the digital age enveloped them, bringing with it the allure of computer games. The virtual realms captivated them, leading them to spend countless hours in online adventures. Ellen and I observed our sons' growing fascination with concern, fully aware of the pitfalls of excessive screen time and the potential for addiction.

Despite our worries, we refused to surrender hope for Hans and Ace. We fervently prayed, seeking God's guidance and the help of the Holy Spirit to navigate this challenging phase. Our commitment to morning and evening worship remained unwavering as we aimed to instill within our sons a steadfast faith capable of withstanding the allure of the digital world.

As our sons transitioned into their teenage years, new trials emerged. The pressures of school and social life intensified their gaming habits, threatening to consume their every waking moment. Ellen and I grappled with the dilemma, yearning for our sons to find balance amidst the digital allure.

Eventually, the time arrived for Hans and Ace to embark on a new adventure: attending boarding school. It was a poignant moment for our family, bidding farewell as they ventured into a new chapter of their lives. Despite the physical distance, our commitment to their spiritual well-being endured. We continued to pray as a family, setting aside time each week to lift up Hans and Ace in prayer using virtual platforms so that we could pray together even when apart.

As time passed, we witnessed a transformation in our sons. Hans and Ace retained their love for computer games but demonstrated newfound maturity and discernment. They began taking breaks from their screens, exploring the outdoors, and pursuing alternative interests. As parents, we found solace in witnessing our sons' growing awareness of the necessity for balance in their lives.

Then, one Saturday evening during our weekly family prayer session, Hans and Ace surprised us by declaring that they had chosen to designate Saturdays as a day of rest and reflection, dedicating the day to God as a Sabbath rest. Additionally, they faithfully gave their tithes every time they received blessings. Ellen and I were overwhelmed with joy, witnessing our sons' commitment to honoring God and prioritizing their spiritual growth.

From the very beginning, since they were born, our family always prayed together, grateful for God's unwavering guidance and support. As Hans and Ace navigated the challenges of the digital age, they did so with a renewed sense of purpose and faith. Together, we embraced each day as an opportunity to journey hand in hand with God, trusting in His strength and grace to lead us forward.

> *"This is my command—be strong and courageous! Do not be afraid or discouraged. For the Lord your God is with you wherever you go."*
>
> Joshua 1:9 - New Living Translation (NLT)

> "Every word, facial expression, gesture, or action on the part of a parent gives the child some message about self-worth. It is sad that so many parents don't realize what messages they are sending."
>
> – Virginia Satir

B. Lessons Learned

Seven lessons that we learned from the story of our family, along with our sons Hans and Ace, highlight several important aspects of parenting spiritually and spiritual growth in the digital age:

1. **Commitment to Faith:** Ellen and I demonstrated an unwavering commitment to introducing our sons to the word of God from a young age, emphasizing the importance of instilling spiritual values early on in a child's life.

   Bible Verse: Proverbs 22:6 (NIV) - "Start children off on the way they should go, and even when they are old they will not turn from it."

2. **Parental Guidance:** Despite the allure of the digital world, as parents, we remained vigilant in monitoring our sons' screen time and guiding them toward a balanced lifestyle. This emphasizes the crucial role that parents play in shaping their children's habits and behaviors, both online and offline.

   Bible Verse: Proverbs 4:23 (NIV) - "Above all else, guard your heart, for everything you do flows from it."

3. **Prayer and Trust:** Throughout our journey, we turned to prayer for guidance and support, highlighting the power of faith and trust in God's plan, especially during challenging times.

   Bible Verse: Philippians 4:6-7 (NIV) - "Do not be anxious about anything, but in every situation, by prayer and petition, with thanksgiving, present your requests to God. And the peace of God, which transcends all understanding, will guard your hearts and your minds in Christ Jesus."

4. **Adaptability:** As our sons grew older and faced new challenges, we adapted our approach to parenting, recognizing the need for flexibility and understanding in navigating the complexities of the digital age.

   Bible Verse: Ecclesiastes 3:1 (NIV) - "There is a time for everything and a season for every activity under the heavens."

5. **Setting Boundaries:** By establishing boundaries, such as designating Saturdays as a day of rest and reflection, we taught our sons the importance of prioritizing spiritual growth and maintaining balance in their lives.

   Bible Verse: Exodus 20:8 (NIV) - "Remember the Sabbath day by keeping it holy."

6. **Leading by Example:** Our own commitment to our faith and our consistent practice of morning and evening worship served as a powerful example for our sons, reinforcing the importance of living out our beliefs in daily life.

   Bible Verse: Matthew 5:16 (NIV) - "In the same way, let your light shine before others, that they may see your good deeds and glorify your Father in heaven."

7. **Communication and Understanding:** Throughout the journey, Ellen and I maintained open communication with our sons, allowing for honest discussions about their struggles and challenges. This lesson highlights the importance of fostering a supportive and understanding environment within the family, where children feel comfortable expressing their concerns and seeking guidance from their parents. By listening empathetically and offering guidance rooted in love and understanding, parents can strengthen their

relationship with their children and effectively navigate the complexities of parenting in the digital age.

Bible Verse: Ephesians 4:29 (NIV) - *"Do not let any unwholesome talk come out of your mouths, but only what is helpful for building others up according to their needs, that it may benefit those who listen."*

Overall, the story underscores the significance of nurturing a strong spiritual foundation within the family and the importance of proactive and intentional parenting in guiding children through the challenges of the digital age.

"The proverb "As you sow, so shall you reap" emphasizes the principle of cause and effect in life. It suggests that the outcomes or consequences of our actions are directly related to the choices we make and the efforts we put forth. In other words, the quality and quantity of what we harvest are determined by the seeds we plant. This timeless wisdom underscores the importance of making wise decisions and investing in positive actions, as they ultimately shape our future and determine the outcomes we experience."

– Jeb and Ellen.

"Don't worry that children never listen to you; worry that they are always watching you."

– Robert Fulghum

Spiritually Focused Parenting in the Digital Era

by: Jazel Martinez - Diaz

In our home, we aim to harness technology as a tool for spiritual growth and education, intentionally creating a balance between digital engagement and faith-based living. By integrating Scripture Songs, Bible stories, and mission content into our routines, we ensure that gadgets serve as instruments for learning, inspiration, and meaningful experiences. Through careful guidance, open discussions, and personal example, we teach our children to approach the digital world responsibly, aligning their screen time with our family's spiritual values and mission.

We frequently use gadgets to cultivate a spiritually enriching environment in our homes. For example, we listen to Scripture Songs together, which helps our children joyfully memorize Bible verses through music. Additionally, our children practice their choir songs using online tutorials, enhancing their experience and making church choir sessions more meaningful. We also watch Bible stories and mission stories, which not only entertain but also inspire values such as kindness, generosity, and faithfulness. This deliberate use of technology ensures that digital tools serve as instruments for spiritual growth rather than sources of distraction.

We are intentional about managing our children's screen time. They are not allowed to use gadgets daily unless we initiate it for specific learning purposes, whether for school or spiritual education. We designate a specific day when they can use devices more freely, but even then, they must ask permission to ensure the content aligns with our family values. This approach teaches them that screen time is a privilege to be used responsibly while we emphasize daily habits like prayer, reflection, and religious education as central to their lives.

We carefully ensure that the digital content our children consume aligns with our spiritual values. Before they engage with any digital media, we preview it either by watching together or beforehand to evaluate its spiritual integrity and filter out anything that contradicts our beliefs. Afterward, we encourage open discussions to reflect on spiritual lessons or challenges the content presents. These discussions help digital media consumption become an extension of their spiritual education.

In addition, we use technology to foster spiritual growth through educational apps and resources. For example, our children are learning sign language and Spanish via online platforms, skills we believe will prepare them for future ministry work. We also teach them to use social media responsibly, emphasizing its potential as a tool for sharing positive, faith-based messages.

Our primary strategy for guiding our children through the distractions of the digital world is leading by example. Recognizing that children often mirror their parents, we strive to be mindful of our own technology use. By staying present and involved in their daily digital activities, we emphasize spiritual values such as self-discipline and responsibility. We frequently discuss staying focused on God and avoiding distractions, incorporating spiritual input into their routines. These conversations help them navigate the digital world while maintaining a strong spiritual foundation.

Love is Spelled as "Time"

by: Kaycee Cerrudo – Ambayec

Living in this digital age brings both challenges and blessings. Many of us fondly recall growing up in simpler times, surrounded by nature and free from the constant buzz of technology. I remember my childhood by the sea, where the shore and trees were our playgrounds, and we spent hours exploring with shells, pebbles, and even bugs, fully immersed in the wonders of the natural world. Today, such experiences may seem foreign to children growing up in a fast-paced, technology-driven world. While nature offers peace and vitality, we now live in an environment of rapid change and constant stimulation, where information—both helpful and harmful—is just a click away, and the allure of social media and smart devices can often lead to anxiety and depression.

We do not believe the digital age is inherently bad, but as parents, we must stay vigilant. The Bible reminds us in John 10:10, "The thief comes only to steal and kill and destroy; I have come that they may have life and have it to the full." If we are not watchful, technology can subtly erode our time with God, robbing us of the joy and purpose that only He can provide. Paul's words in Philippians 4:8 serve as a guide: "Finally, brethren, whatever is true, whatever is noble, whatever is right, whatever is pure, whatever is lovely, whatever is admirable—if anything is excellent or praiseworthy—think about such things."

As a family, we prioritize intentional time together, including morning and evening worship. We ensure our daughter feels loved and valued by investing in quality time with her, recognizing that many parents today allow gadgets to substitute for the attention children truly need. While toys and devices may entertain temporarily, nothing compares to the lasting impact of genuine, shared moments. As the Bible teaches in 1 Timothy 3:4-5, our family is our first ministry. By God's grace, we dedicate time to activities such as outdoor worship, beach trips, camping, and simple indoor pastimes like puzzles, crafts, and games. We also involve our daughter in household chores, teaching her practical skills like tidying her bed, preparing meals, and baking.

In today's world, completely avoiding gadgets is unrealistic, but we are deliberate about how and when our daughter uses them. She does not have her own device but uses the family desktop for specific purposes like watching Bible stories, learning Scripture songs, or participating in online Midweek Prayers. We have also chosen not to have a television in our home. Her screen time is limited to 3-5 hours per week, always supervised, and with a focus on spiritual growth.

As parents, it is essential that we model the behavior we want our children to emulate. The rules we set must align with our actions so we remain disciplined in our use of technology. For example, we have a family rule against using phones at the dining table, as we believe mealtime should be dedicated to connection. Parenting demands self-denial and sacrifice, and we rely on Jesus for the strength to meet this calling. Philippians 4:13 reminds us, "I can do all things through Christ who strengthens me."

What we focus on shapes us, which is why it is crucial to guard ourselves and our children against distractions that can pull us away from God. Deuteronomy 6:5-7 instructs us to love the Lord with all our hearts and to diligently teach His words to our children throughout daily life. To effectively teach these truths, we must first internalize them ourselves. As Ellen G. White wrote in Education (p. 187), "Our instruction to them will have only the weight of influence given it by our own example and spirit." While we are far from perfect, we trust in the promise of Philippians 1:6: "He who began a good work in you will carry it on to completion."

Though we do our best to guard and guide our daughter, we understand that she will ultimately make her own choices, influenced by her environment. Yet, we rest in the assurance that God is faithful, and we surrender her to Him. The best thing we can do, as parents, is to fervently pray for her, trusting that God will lead her on the path of righteousness.

CHAPTER X

Moving Forward

In navigating the complex landscape of parenting spiritually in the digital age, we find ourselves confronted with an array of challenges and opportunities. As parents, we strive to guide our children towards a deeper understanding of their spiritual selves amidst the constant influx of digital stimuli. Our journey in this regard is one of continuous learning and adaptation, where we must remain vigilant yet open-minded.

In "Moving Forward," we are reminded of the importance of fostering a sense of mindfulness and intentionality in our approach to parenting in the digital world. It is crucial for us to cultivate an environment where our children can develop a strong spiritual foundation, even amidst the distractions and pressures of the online realm. We recognize that this requires a delicate balance – one that acknowledges the benefits of technology while also emphasizing the value of traditional spiritual practices.

As we move forward on this path, we commit ourselves to being proactive in shaping our children's digital experiences. We strive to engage in meaningful conversations about the impact of technology on their spiritual well-being and to provide them with the tools they need to navigate this space with integrity and discernment. Moreover, we recognize the importance of leading by example, demonstrating through our own actions the value of prioritizing spiritual growth in an increasingly digital world.

In essence, our journey of parenting spiritually in the digital age is one of constant evolution and adaptation. By embracing the principles of "Moving Forward," we can navigate this terrain with confidence and grace, empowering our children to thrive spiritually amidst the challenges of the digital world.

> *"Commit your works to the Lord [submit and trust them to Him], And your plans will succeed [if you respond to His will and guidance]."*

Proverbs 16:3 - Amplified Bible (AMP)

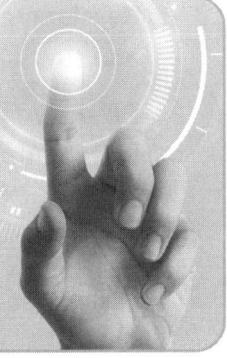

> *"When you hold your baby in your arms the first time, and you think of all the things you can say and do to influence him, it's a tremendous responsibility. What you do with him can influence not only him, but everyone he meets and not for a day or a month or a year but for time and eternity."*
>
> – Rose Kennedy

A. Building On Spiritual Foundations

As parents, we fully grasp the profound significance of our role in nurturing and guiding our children, understanding it to be one of life's most enriching and fulfilling relationships. However, amidst the relentless whirlwind of school drop-offs, work obligations, and the everyday demands of managing a household, it's all too common to find ourselves grappling with a sense of being stretched thin and overwhelmed.

Furthermore, in this modern era dominated by technology, the task of parenting can feel even more daunting. With screens infiltrating nearly every aspect of our lives, from education to entertainment, we're faced with unprecedented challenges in raising our children with values that align with our beliefs and principles.

In light of these complexities, we feel compelled to share some invaluable insights on parenting from a biblical perspective. Drawing wisdom from timeless teachings, we seek to offer practical guidance and spiritual grounding to navigate the maze of modern parenthood.

Here are some principles to incorporate into our parenting journey of establishing, nurturing, and building spiritual foundations.

1. **Value Playtime:** Acknowledge the significance of play in our children's lives. It's not merely leisure; it's crucial for their holistic development. Play fosters learning, prevents disciplinary issues, and strengthens the parent-child bond (Ephesians 6:4).

2. **Effective Communication:** Engage in meaningful conversations with our children, maintaining eye contact and using gentle touches. Offer clear instructions without overwhelming them. Non-verbal cues like hugs and smiles further enhance communication (Proverbs 1:8-9).

3. **Nurture Mind and Body:** Provide nutritious meals, model healthy eating habits, and encourage physical activity. Limit screen time and create opportunities for learning and exploration beyond digital realms (Ephesians 5:29).

4. **Be the Primary Source of Guidance:** Encourage our children to ask questions, fostering trust and openness. Honest responses create a foundation of mutual respect, preventing them from adopting unsafe behaviors (Proverbs 1:2-4).

5. **Understand Child Development:** As parents, we are the experts on our children. Understanding their physical, intellectual, social, emotional, and moral development is essential for providing tailored support (Proverbs 22:6).

6. **Celebrate Individuality:** Embrace and support our children's unique interests and talents. Spend quality time with each child daily, avoiding comparisons and praising their individual qualities (Isaiah 11:6).

7. **Create a Harmonious Household:** Establish routines and rules that promote safety and cooperation. Model good behavior and enforce family guidelines effectively (Deuteronomy 6:1-9).

8. **Prioritize Self-care:** Recognize the importance of our own well-being in effective parenting. Eat healthily, get enough rest, and seek support when needed (1 Corinthians 6:19).

9. **Foster Family Bonding:** Make time for shared activities and discussions to strengthen familial ties and promote a sense of belonging (Mark 5:19).

10. **Teach Moral Values:** Guide our children in understanding right from wrong, laying the foundation for their moral compass (Matthew 7:12).

By incorporating these principles into our parenting journey, we can navigate the challenges of raising spiritually grounded children in a digital age while nurturing their growth and well-being.

"All children are foolish, but firm correction will make them change."

Proverbs 22:15
- Contemporary English Version (CEV)

"The goal of human life is to beautify the soul through goodness and virtue and to make it worthy of offering to God Who is the Beautiful."

– Seyyed Hosssein Nasr in The Heart of Wisdom

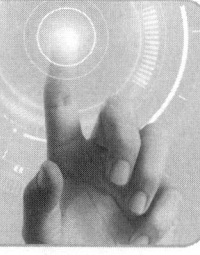

B. Parenting As A Lifelong Spiritual Quest

When we consider "parenting as a lifelong spiritual quest," we're embracing the notion that raising children encompasses more than just fulfilling practical duties; it's a deeply meaningful spiritual journey that spans our entire lives. Let's delve into each aspect:

1. **Parenting:** As parents, our primary role is to nurture and guide our children through their journey of growth and development. This involves providing them with love, care, and support as they navigate the complexities of life.

2. **Lifelong:** Parenthood isn't a temporary phase; it's an ongoing commitment that evolves alongside our children. Even as they mature into adults, we continue to influence their lives, offering unwavering support and guidance whenever they need it.

3. **Spiritual:** The spiritual aspect of parenting encompasses our beliefs, values, and practices that give meaning and purpose to our lives. It involves instilling moral values, fostering generosity, promoting love for one another, teaching forgiveness, nurturing empathy and compassion, and guiding our children to cultivate a profound connection with our Lord God and Savior, Jesus Christ. Furthermore, we prioritize ensuring that they are firmly connected to His teachings, grounded in the word of God, and guided by the Holy Spirit to attain knowledge and wisdom.

4. **Quest:** Parenting can be likened to a quest—a continuous journey of self-discovery and growth. It's a pursuit of personal enlightenment and fulfillment, where we strive to deepen our understanding of ourselves, our children, and the world around us. Along this quest, we learn, evolve, and forge deeper connections with our children and ourselves.

In essence, viewing parenting as a lifelong spiritual quest encourages us to explore the profound depths of our values, beliefs, and purpose as we nurture and support the growth and development of the next generation. It transcends the mere practicalities of caregiving, inviting us to embark on a sacred journey of self-discovery, connection, and enlightenment alongside our children.

> *"We don't enjoy discipline when we get it. It is painful. But later, after we have learned our lesson from it, we will enjoy the peace that comes from doing what is right."*
>
> Hebrews 12:11 - Easy-to-Read Version (ERV)

> *"The choice of a life companion should be such as best to secure physical, mental, and spiritual well-being for parents and for their children—such as will enable both parents and children to bless their fellow men and to honor their Creator."*
>
> – Adventist Home p. 45.3

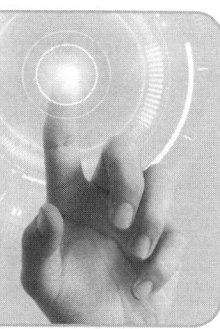

C. Encouraging Spiritual Growth In Children

Encouraging spiritual growth in our children is a vital aspect of parenting that involves developing their whole being, nurturing their faith, values, and understanding of spiritual concepts. Here's how we can approach this important task in order for us as parents to ensure the spiritual growth of our children:

1. **Exploring Scripture together:** Reading and discussing Bible stories and passages with our children can provide them with a solid foundation in Christian beliefs and values. Engaging in age-appropriate Bible study sessions, devotions, or family worship

times allows our children to ask questions, express their thoughts, and deepen their understanding of God's word.

> *"Blessed is the one who reads aloud the words of this prophecy, and blessed are those who hear, and who keep what is written in it, for the time is near. " - Revelation 1:3 (ESV)*

5. **Teaching Discernment:** In a digital world filled with various influences, we teach our children to discern between what is beneficial and what may lead them astray spiritually. We encourage critical thinking and reliance on biblical wisdom.

> *"Your word is a lamp to my feet and a light to my path." - Psalm 119:105 (ESV)*

6. **Modeling Faith:** We understand that our actions speak louder than words. By modeling our faith in our digital interactions, we exemplify the values and principles we seek to instill in our children.

> *"But as for me and my house, we will serve the Lord." - Joshua 24:15b (ESV)*

7. **Encouraging Connection:** While digital technology can sometimes hinder genuine connection, we use it as a tool to foster meaningful relationships within our family and community. We prioritize spending quality time together and engaging in discussions about faith and spirituality.

> *"And let us consider how to stir up one another to love and good works, not neglecting to meet together, as is the habit of some, but encouraging one another, and all the more as you see the Day drawing near." - Hebrews 10:24-25 (ESV)*

8. **Practicing Prayer:** In the midst of digital distractions, we emphasize the importance of prayer as a means of staying connected to God and seeking His guidance in our daily lives, including our digital interactions.

"Do not be anxious about anything, but in everything by prayer and supplication with thanksgiving let your requests be made known to God." - Philippians 4:6 (ESV)

In essence, parenting spiritually in the digital world requires intentional effort to integrate biblical principles into our children's digital experiences. By exploring scripture together, teaching discernment, modeling faith, encouraging connection, and practicing prayer, we strive to nurture their spiritual growth in a technology-driven society.

"Remember to warn your children when they do something wrong. If you punish them with a stick, you will not kill them. Punishment may save them from death."

Proverbs 23:13-14 – EasyEnglish Bible (EASY)

"With us as parents and as Christians, it rests to give our children the right direction. They are to be carefully, wisely, and tenderly guided into paths of Christlike ministry. We are under a sacred covenant with God to rear our children for His service. To surround them with such influences as shall lead them to choose a life of service and to give them the training needed is our first duty."

– Adventist Home p. 484.1

SUMMARY

Recap of Key Points:

1. **Understanding the Digital Landscape:** Acknowledges the complexity and dynamism of the digital world, highlighting both its opportunities and challenges. It stresses the need for vigilance, critical thinking, and proactive action to address ethical, social, and political implications while harnessing digital technology for positive change.

2. **Balancing Technology Use:** Recognizes the negative impacts of technology on parenting, such as screen time battles and digital addiction, emphasizing the importance of balancing technology's benefits with mitigating its negative effects for the well-being of children.

3. **Prioritizing Connection and Communication:** Emphasizes the essential role of genuine connection and open communication between parents and children in navigating the digital world. It underscores the transformative impact of meaningful interactions in fostering emotional well-being and resilience.

4. **Anchoring Parenting in Biblical Principles:** Advocates for grounding parenting approaches in biblical values, such as setting boundaries, modeling ethical behavior, and fostering a Christ-centered worldview. It highlights the importance of instilling moral discernment and spiritual resilience in children to navigate digital challenges.

5. **Digital Discipleship and Family Devotions:** Highlights the significance of digital discipleship and family devotions in nurturing children's faith within a technological society. It suggests integrating digital resources with traditional practices and modeling discernment in digital habits to foster spiritual growth.

6. **Creating a God-honoring Digital Environment:** Proposes establishing a digital covenant within families rooted in the

Christian faith to cultivate a nurturing and God-honoring digital environment. It emphasizes the importance of setting boundaries, fostering accountability, and seeking divine guidance in digital stewardship.

7. **Empowering Children Spiritually:** Focuses on equipping children with the tools and foundation to live out their faith daily, both online and offline, through spiritual practices, biblical teaching, and community support. It aims to raise children who are deeply connected to God and shine His light in the digital sphere.

8. **Promoting Compassion and Service:** Advocates for guiding children to practice compassion, kindness, and service in their online interactions, empowering them to make a positive difference in the digital world. It underscores the role of modeling compassionate behavior and promoting digital citizenship.

9. **Constant Evolution and Adaptation:** Acknowledges parenting in the digital age as a journey of constant evolution and adaptation, requiring confidence, grace, and a commitment to moving forward while nurturing children's spiritual growth amidst digital challenges.

10. **Lifelong Spiritual Quest:** Views parenting as a lifelong spiritual quest, inviting parents to explore and deepen their values, beliefs, and purpose alongside their children. It emphasizes the sacred journey of self-discovery, connection, and enlightenment in nurturing the next generation spiritually.

Ultimately, parenting in the digital age is depicted as a sacred journey—a profound and ongoing spiritual exploration that entails not only guiding our children but also delving deeper into our own values, beliefs, and purpose. It's a journey marked by continuous growth and adaptation, where we, as parents, are tasked with navigating the complexities of the digital landscape while being guided by the timeless wisdom found in Scripture. This journey necessitates a steadfast commitment to advancement, moving forward with a blend of confidence and grace.

In conclusion, this book advocates for a holistic approach to parenting in the digital era—an approach that integrates biblical principles, fosters meaningful connections and equips our children with the necessary tools to navigate the digital realm with integrity, compassion, and unwavering faith. By embracing this comprehensive approach, we position ourselves to raise children deeply rooted in their relationship with God, emanating His love and wisdom in an increasingly digitized and interconnected society. It is imperative that our children remain connected to the profound love of our Heavenly Father, grounded in the principles of God's Word, and guided by the teachings of our Lord God and Saviour Jesus Christ through His grace, as well as the wisdom of truth provided by the Holy Spirit.

LOVE LETTER FOR PARENTS

Dear Parents,

I hope this letter finds you and your family in good health and high spirits. As parents navigating the challenges of raising children in the digital age, I want to extend my heartfelt encouragement and support to you. Parenting in today's digital world comes with its own set of unique challenges, but it also offers tremendous opportunities for growth, connection, and spiritual enrichment.

First and foremost, I want to commend you for your dedication to nurturing your children's spiritual development amidst the distractions and complexities of the digital landscape. Your commitment to instilling biblical values, fostering meaningful connections, and guiding your children in their faith journey is truly admirable.

I understand that it can sometimes feel overwhelming to balance the demands of technology with the desire to raise spiritually grounded children. The constant influx of digital information, social media pressures, and online influences can make it challenging to maintain a sense of spiritual focus and direction within the family.

However, I want to reassure you that you are not alone in this journey. As fellow parents, we are all navigating these uncharted waters together, learning and growing along the way. It's important to remember that you are doing a remarkable job, even on the days when it may feel like you're falling short.

In times of doubt or uncertainty, I encourage you to lean on your faith and trust in God's guidance. Seek solace in prayer, draw wisdom from Scripture, and find strength in the support of your faith community. Remember that God has entrusted you with the precious responsibility of shaping your children's hearts and minds, and He will equip you with the tools and resources you need to fulfill this calling.

It's also essential to prioritize open communication and meaningful connections within your family. Take the time to engage in heartfelt conversations with your children, listen to their concerns, and share your own experiences and insights. Create opportunities for shared experiences, whether it's through family devotions, service projects, or simply spending quality time together offline.

As you continue on this journey of parenting spiritually in the digital world, I encourage you to be gentle with yourself and with your children. Embrace imperfection, celebrate small victories, and extend grace to yourself and others along the way. Remember that it's okay to seek help and support when needed, whether from trusted friends, family members, or professional counselors.

In closing, I want to affirm your dedication and perseverance as parents striving to raise children who are deeply rooted in their relationship with God. Your efforts are making a significant impact, and your love and guidance are shaping the hearts and minds of the next generation in profound ways. May God bless you abundantly as you continue to walk this path of parenting with faith, courage, and grace.

"I pray that the Lord Jesus Christ will continue to be very kind to you all. I pray that God's love will be with you. And I pray that the Holy Spirit will help you to serve each other as friends."

2 Corinthians 13:14 - EasyEnglish Bible (EASY)

With warm regards and prayers,
Jeb J. Bersabal, MBA, PhD (candidate)

REFERENCE

Scripture use:

Chapter

Intro   Proverbs 22:6 - The Message (MSG)
Titus 2:7-8 - Amplified Bible, Classic Edition (AMPC)

1.   Proverbs 29:17 New International Version (NIV)
Proverbs 4:23 - New International Version (NIV)
Psalm 119:105 - New International Version (NIV)
Romans 12:2 - New International Version (NIV)

2.   Colossians 4:6 – EasyEnglish Bible (EASY)
Deuteronomy 6:5-8 - New Century Version (NCV)
Ephesians 6:4 - Living Bible (TLB)
Proverbs 3:11, 12 - Good News Translation (GNT)

3.   2 Timothy 3:16-17 - Living Bible (TLB)
Colossians 3:2 - New Life Version (NLV)
1 Corinthians 6:12 – New International Version (NIV)
Romans 5:3-5 - Living Bible (TLB)

4.   Micah 6:8 - The Message (MSG)
Philippians 4:6-7 - Living Bible (TLB)
1 Timothy 4:8 - Easy-to-Read Version (ERV)
Hebrews 4:12 - New International Version (NIV)

5.   Proverbs 1:8-9 - EasyEnglish Bible (EASY)
Isaiah 61:1 - New Life Version (NLV)
Deuteronomy 4:9 - EasyEnglish Bible (EASY)
Colossians 3:16 - Contemporary English Version (CEV)

6.   Deuteronomy 31:6 - New Life Version (NLV)
Ecclesiastes 3:1 - Evangelical Heritage Version (EHV)
Galatians 6:1- Common English Bible (CEB)
James 4:7-10 - The Message (MSG)

7. James 4:17 - New Life Version (NLV)
    Psalm 1:1-2 - Amplified Bible, Classic Edition (AMPC)
    Colossians 3:20 - Good News Translation (GNT)
    Colossians 3:12-14 - New International Version (NIV)

8. Proverbs 29:15 - Easy-to-Read Version (ERV)
    James 2:17- Living Bible (TLB)
    Isaiah 58:10 - Living Bible (TLB)
    Ephesians 4:32 - New International Version (NIV)

9. Joshua 1:9 - New Living Translation (NLT)

10. Proverbs 16:3 - Amplified Bible (AMP)
    Hebrews 12:11 - Easy-to-Read Version (ERV)
    Proverbs 22:15 - Contemporary English Version (CEV)
    Proverbs 23:13-14 – EasyEnglish Bible (EASY)

Other Scripture Use:

1 Corinthians 10:13

1 Corinthians 10:31

1 Corinthians 6:12

1 Corinthians 6:19

2 Corinthians 10:5

2 Corithians 13:14

1 John 4:7

1 Thessalonians 5:11

1 Thessalonians 5:16-18

1 Timothy 3:4-5

1 Timothy 4:8

1 Timothy 4:12

2 Timothy 3:16-17

Colossians 3:2

Colossians 3:12

Colossians 3:12-14

Colossians 3:16

Colossians 3:17

Colossians 3:20

Colossians 4:6

Deuteronomy 31:6

Deuteronomy 4:9

Deuteronomy 6:1-9

Deuteronomy 6:5-8

Deuteronomy 6:6-7

Ecclesiastes 3:1

Ecclesiastes 3:22

Ecclesiastes 4:9-10

Ephesians 4:29

Ephesians 4:32

Ephesians 5:1-2

Ephesians 5:15-16

Ephesians 5:15-17

Ephesians 5:29

Ephesians 6:4

Ephesians 6:10-18

Exodus 20:8

Galatians 5:22-23

Galatians 6:1

Galatians 6:10

Genesis 1:28

Hebrews 4:12

Hebrews 10:23

Hebrews 10:24-25

Hebrews 12:11

Isaiah 11:6

Isaiah 58:10

Isaiah 61:1

James 1:5

James 2:14-17

James 2:17

James 4:7-10

James 4:17

John 10:10

John 13:34-35

Joshua 1:9

Mark 10:45

Mark 5:19

Matthew 5:16

Matthew 5:44

Matthew 7:12

Matthew 11:28-30

Matthew 22:39

Matthew 28:19

Micah 6:8

Philippians 1:6

Philippians 2:3-4

Philippians 2:4

Philippians 4:6-7

Philippians 4:8

Philippians 4:9

Philippians 4:13

Proverbs 1:2-4

Proverbs 1:8-9

Proverbs 2:6

Proverbs 3:11, 12

Proverbs 4:7

Proverbs 4:23

Proverbs 4:25-27

Proverbs 16:3

Proverbs 16:24

Proverbs 22:6

Proverbs 22:15

Proverbs 23:13-14

Proverbs 27:17

Proverbs 29:15

Proverbs 29:17

Psalm 1:1-2

Psalm 90:12

Psalm 119:11

Psalm 119:105

Romans 5:3-5

Romans 12:2

Titus 2:7-8

Bible Version Use:

AMP -   Amplified Bible (AMP)

AMPC -   Amplified Bible, Classic Edition (AMPC)

CEB -   Common English Bible (CEB)

CEV -   Contemporary English Version (CEV)

EASY -   EasyEnglish Bible (EASY)

EHV -   Evangelical Heritage Version (EHV)

ERV -   Easy-to-Read Version (ERV)

GNT -   Good News Translation (GNT)

MSG -   The Message (MSG)

NCV -   New Century Version (NCV)

NIV -   New International Version (NIV)

NLT -   New Living Translation (NLT)

NLV -   New Life Version (NLV)

TLB -   Living Bible (TLB)

EasyEnglish Bible (EASY)

Evangelical Heritage Version (EHV)

Easy-to-Read Version (ERV)

Good News Translation (GNT)

The Message (MSG)

New Century Version (NCV)

New International Version (NIV)

New Living Translation (NLT)

New Life Version (NLV)

Living Bible (TLB)

Quotations by:

Adventist Home	Messages to Young People
Billy Graham	Michael Rutter
Brooke Hampton	Nicole O'Dell
Dr Lucy Russell	Nishan Panwar
Ed Japlit	Os Guinness
Elaine Halligan	Review and Herald
Ellen G. White	Robert Fulghum
Germany Kent	Rose Kennedy
Henri Frederic Amiel	Ruston
Jabez Ministry	Seyyed Hosssein Nasr
Jeb J. Bersabal	Testimonies for the Church
Jesse Duplantis	Unknown
Joyce Meyer	Virginia Satir
Lisa Wingate	Wayne Dyer & Ed Japlit
L.R. Knost, author	Whitney Wolfe Herd
Max Lucado	

Book:

Arredondo, M. (2016). *Parenting as a Spiritual Practice: Incorporating the Wisdom of World Traditions.* Rowman & Littlefield.

Bandura, A. (1977). *Social Learning Theory.* Prentice Hall.

Blair, S. L., & Umberson, D. (2017). *Family Relationships and Health.* In Handbook of the Sociology of Health, Illness, and Healing (pp. 109-123). Springer.

Eisenberg, N., Spinrad, T. L., & Knafo-Noam, A. (2016). *Prosocial Development.* In Handbook of Child Psychology and Developmental Science (pp. 1-48). John Wiley & Sons.

Fiese, B. H., Tomcho, T. J., Douglas, M., Josephs, K., Poltrock, S., & Baker, T. (2002). A Review of 50 Years of Research on Naturally Occurring Family Routines and Rituals: Cause for Celebration?. *Journal of Family Psychology,* 16(4), 381–390.

Gershoff, E. T. (2013). *Spanking and Child Development:* We Know Enough Now to Stop Hitting Our Children. Child Development Perspectives, 7(3), 133–137.

Gottlieb, M. (2011). *The Spirituality of Parenting: Connecting Heart and Soul.* SkyLight Paths Publishing.

Hinduja, S., & Patchin, J. W. (2015). *Bullying beyond the Schoolyard: Preventing and Responding to Cyberbullying* (2nd ed.). Corwin Press.

Hinduja, S., & Patchin, J. W. (2020). *Words Wound: Delete Cyberbullying and Make Kindness Go Viral.* Free Spirit Publishing.

Jones, S. L., & Butman, R. E. (2011). *Modern Psychotherapies: A Comprehensive Christian Appraisal* (2nd ed.). IVP Academic.

Katz, L. F., & Gottman, J. M. (1996). *Marital Conflict and Children's Adjustment: Developmental Psychopathology Perspective.* In J. A. Grych & F. D. Fincham (Eds.), *Interparental Conflict and Child Development:* Theory, Research, and Applications (pp. 129- 156). Cambridge University Press.

McLeod, S. (2017). *Active Listening. Simply Psychology.* Retrieved from https://www.simplypsychology.org/active-listening.html

Miller, L., & Kelley, B. (Eds.). (2018). *Parenting for Peace: Raising the Next Generation of Peacemakers.* North Atlantic Books.

Ponciano, L., Toma, C. L., & Guitton, M. J. (2019). *Parenting in the digital age: Control and parental behaviors in times of change.* Journal of Applied Developmental Psychology, 62, 173- 184.

Rohner, R. P. (2004). The Parental "Acceptance-Rejection Syndrome": Universal Correlates of Perceived Rejection. American Psychologist, 59(8), 830–840.

Shay Bilchik - *10 Tips for Biblical Parenting* | New Life

Simons, R. L., & Conger, R. D. (2007). *Linking Family Processes and Academic Competence Among Rural African American Youths.* Journal of Marriage and Family, 69 (2), 460–474.

Tan, S. Y., & Tan, L. H. (2012). *Counseling and Christianity: Five Approaches.* Baker Academic.

Periodical:

American Academy of Pediatrics

Bandura, 1977

Blair & Umberson, 2017

Common Sense Media

Edutopia

Eisenberg et al., 2016

Fiese et al., 2002

Gershoff, 2013

HealthyChildren.org

Katz & Gottman, 1996

McLeod, 2017

National PTA

Parents.com

Ponciano, et al., 2019.

Psychology Today

Rohner, 2004

Simons & Conger, 2007

The Guardian

The New York Times

UNESCO

Website:

https://cyberbullying.org

https://thearkgroup.org/how-can-parents-effectively-guide-their-children-through-the-digital-age

https://www.icactaskforce.org/internetsafety https://www.pacer.org/bullying/info/cyberbullying

https://www.spiritrestoration.org/spirituality/how-to-raise-a-spiritual-child/#google_vignette

https://www.stopbullying.gov/resources/get-help-now

God Bless us all!

Code Tag: 7313-7-13312851357

J2024E03B29